Tennessee Trivia No. 1
A compilation of short articles about Persons, Places and Events in the Volunteer State

Jerry H. Summers

Waldenhouse Publishers, inc.
Walden, Tennessee

Tennessee Trivia No. 1: A compilation of short articles about persons, places and events in the Volunteer State.

Copyright 2020. Jerry H. Summers 1941. All rights reserved. No part of this book may be reproduced in any form or by any electronic or mechanical means including information storage and retrieval systems, without permission in writing from the publisher. The only exception is by a reviewer, who may quote short excerpts in a review.

Published by Waldenhouse Publishers, Inc.
100 Clegg Street, Signal Mountain, Tennessee 37377 USA
888-222-8228 www.waldenhouse.com
Printed in the United States of America
Editing, Type and Design by Karen Paul Stone
ISBN: 978-1-947589-29-2
Library of Congress Control Number: 2020943360

    Sixty-seven short stories with forty-nine photographs compiled by lawyer-historian, Jerry Summers, about lesser known but interesting persons, places and events in the Volunteer state, Tennessee, in the southeastern United States of America.

HIS036120 HISTORY / United States / State & Local / South
HIS036060 HISTORY / United States / 20th Century
HIS054000 HISTORY / Social History

    Proceeds from the sale of *Tennessee Trivia* will go to Orange Grove Center (OGC), a 501(c)(3) Charitable organization under the Internal Revenue status. Copies of *Tennessee Trivia* can be purchased directly from Orange Grove Center, 615 Derby Street, Chattanooga, Tennessee, 37404 – or – www.orangegrovecenter.org

Dedication

To the staff, parents and volunteers of
Orange Grove Center in Chattanooga, Tennessee
who tirelessly work to provide worthwhile life experiences
to people with intellectual and developmental disabilities

Table of Contents

Dedication	3
Preface	9
Acknowledgments	11
Introduction	13
Section 1 – PERSONS	15
Grace Moore – Tennessee Nightingale	15
Tom Mix & Jobyna Raulston-Arlens – South Pittsburgh's Silent Movie Stars	18
Dinah Shore – Winchester & McMinnville's Movie Star	21
Peggy Dow – Athens, Tennessee Movie Star	24
Nellie Kenyon – Chattanooga News Reporter Extraordinaire	27
Drue Smith – Woman Pioneer In Journalism And Media	29
Ralph McGill – Soddy's Civil Rights Advocate	32
John N. Popham, III – Chattanooga's Iconic Newspaperman	35
Charles Bartlett – Pulitzer Prize Winner	38
Anna Mae Clift – The Soddy Girl and the Memphis Belle	41
Martin W. Littleton – Rags to Riches lawyer	44
Judge Sue K. Hicks – A Boy Named Sue	46
John R. Neal – Scopes Eccentric Lawyer	48
Al Capone – Monteagle's Most Notorious Visitor	51
Herschel P. Franks – Longest Serving State Judge	54
Frank W. Wilson – Federal District Judge Number One	57
David McKendree Key – Chattanooga's 1st Federal District Judge	60
Tennessee's U.S. Supreme Court Justices	62
Ellis K. Meacham – Author and Judge	69
Sgt. Alvin York – When Sergeant York Came to Chattanooga	71

Ray Eugene Duke – Whitwell's Medal of Honor Hero	73
Raymond H. Cooley – Medal of Honor - Dunlap	75
Charles "Duke" Pearman – Korean War POW	77
Raymond Prater – Audie Murphy's Chattanooga Connection	79
William Emerson Brock, Sr. – A Democrat in the Brock Family	82
Carey Estes Kefauver – Chattanooga's Congressman and Senator	84
Nathan Lynn Bachman – Chattanooga's Beloved Senator	88
Thomas Jefferson Anderson – Baylor School's Presidential Candidate	90
Jim Cummings, I.D. Beasley & Walter "Pete" Haynes – Tennessee's Unholy Trinity	92
John R. Neal – Scopes Eccentric lawyer	97
Pioneer Women Attorneys	96
Bryon De La Beckweth – Signal Mountain's Infamous Resident	98
Charles Lindbergh – When "Lucky Lindy" Landed in Chattanooga	101
Phillip R. Love – The Other Plane and Pilot at Marr Field	103
Jim T. Fitzgerald – South Pittsburg's Sound Barrier Breaker	105
Joseph C. White – Chattanooga's Tuskegee Airman	107
Harry G. Porter – Daredevil & Aviator	109
Joe Engel – Barnum of Baseball	112
Willie Six – Sewanee's African American Gentleman	115
Lon Varnell – Sewanee's Coaching Showman	117
The Majors – Tennessee Football Family	119
John Wilkes Booth – At Sewanee	121
Dr. William Gorgas – And the Panama Canal	124

Section 2 – PLACES

Burritt College – Pioneer of the Cumberlands	127
Beersheba Springs – Mountain Resort	130
Chattanooga's Law School	133

American Temperance University – Harriman, Tennessee	135
Camp Crossville – World War II	138
The Crosses at Sewanee	141
Marr Field – How Marr Field became Lovell Field	143
Chamberlain Field – Turkey Day Football	146
Chattanooga Cherokees – Chattanooga's Professional Football Team	149
Roller Derby – Chattanooga's Skaters	152
Stock Car Racing History – Chattanooga's Contributors	155
Wrestling or "Rassling" in Chattanooga	158
Soap Box Derby – Chattanooga's Non-Motorized NASCAR	161
Sewanee Football – SEC to Division III	165

Section 3 – EVENTS

Chattanooga's Cotton Ball	167
Tennessee Adoption Scandal	169
Copperhill-McCaysville Adoption Scandal	171
Chattanooga Divorce Mill Scandal	173
Moonshine Feud – Daisy Mountain #1	175
Moonshine Feud – Daisy Mountain #2	178
Battle of Athens – McMinn County War	180
Christmas Night Massacre – South Pittsburg	183
Whitwell Mine Disaster	185
Bloody Bledsoe County	188
Conclusion	191
The Author	192

Preface

Although I have lived all but seven years in the State of Tennessee, I have recently become more educated and hopefully knowledgeable of the rich history of our state since it was settled and became the 16th state to become a part of our country on June 1, 1796.

I have tried to pick out the unusual personalities and events to fill in a few gaps of known and lesser known parts of our state's history.

Acknowledgments

Without the support and encouragement of both the editorial staffs of *Chattanooga Times Free-Press* and *Chattanoogan.com*, I probably would not have ventured into the field of journalism at the retirement age of my early 70s. I do not profess to be a published writer and my grammatical mistakes often are embarrassing to some of my friends and welcome critics.

Fortunately, there are folks who have followed behind me and helped clean up my most serious mistakes. Without the help of my paralegal, Nick Walker, and my receptionist, Joy Hayes, who have suffered through the agony of attempts to decipher my sometimes unreadable handwriting in my first drafts, I say thank you for all of your efforts and understanding.

One of the most enjoyable results of my writings has been the comments of readers who not only criticize and thank me for writing something about a friend, relative, or event, but who have also, on occasion, made a recommendation as to another possible topic that I might look into for a future article. Fortunately, the criticism has been limited.

My first career as a trial lawyer of 53 years experience in the courtroom is not over, but the joy of researching and writing about my county, state and the South has made the transition to part-time lawyer much easier.

Introduction

Several years ago, I started writing infrequent articles in the *Chattanooga Times Free-Press* on local historical events in the Perspective Section under Editor Chris Vass and with local writer and financial advisor Mickey Robbins. I subsequently starting writing two columns a week in John Wilson's website newspaper *Chattanoogan.com* under the Happenings Column and broadened the schedule of topics to include the sister states of Alabama and Georgia. These columns deal with the topics of persons, places and things in those states as well as the Volunteer State of Tennessee.

The history of the State of Tennessee includes many famous individuals and events. In this publication, I have tried to accumulate stories about lesser known persons and happenings that add colorful stories of some of those personalities and events.

This book is a compilation of only a small number of the Tennessee topics as the interesting list of subjects began to mushroom. If there is sufficient interest in the contents, I hope to do other volumes that will include Tennessee, Alabama, and Georgia.

More importantly, the proceeds from the sale of the books will benefit one of my favorite charities, Orange Grove Center.

PERSONS

Grace Moore – Tennessee Nightingale

Interred amongst Chattanooga's notables at Forest Hills Cemetery in St. Elmo is a native of Slabtown (part of Del Rio) Tennessee, in Cocke County, "Mary Willie Grace Moore." Although there is a discrepancy as to her actual date of birth being in 1898 or 1901, she is remembered as Grace Moore, an outstanding actress and singer in the 1930's-1940's.

At an early age she moved with her parents to Jellico, Tennessee, north of Knoxville. Even though her ambitions to be a singer were disapproved by her father, Colonel Richard Moore, she continued to develop her talents. In 1928, she debuted at the Metropolitan Opera House in New York City.

After she left Tennessee to pursue a joint singing and acting career, her parents moved to Chattanooga. Grace's brother, James Moore, Sr. and other members of the family became owners and executive officers of the Loveman's Department Store located on the corner of 8th and Market Street in Chattanooga. The Moores were staunch supporters of the University of Tennessee, and family members served several terms on the University's Board of Trustees.

It was through this relationship that many of the costumes and other memorabilia of Grace were donated to the University of Tennessee and stored at the Frank H. McClung Museum on the U.T.K. campus. Many of those items had previously been given to the Museum of the City of New York upon Mrs. Moore's tragic and unexpected death in 1947. Prior to her demise, her career had been one of meteoric rise to the top of the entertainment world.

Grace made her Broadway debut in the 1920 musical "Hitchey-Koo" written by the renowned Jerome Kern. She also appeared in two of Irving Berlin's four "Music Box Revues." Not content with just performing in musicals, she studied in France to become an opera singer. Her first role at the Metropolitan Opera in New York was in the role of Mimi in Puccini's, "La Boheme."

Grace Moore

In a career that was of international scope, she appeared before royalty in Europe and during the 1930's sang operas in the French, Spanish, German, Italian and English languages. During World War II, she entertained America troops abroad with the U.S.O. in Europe.

Her movie career in Hollywood was also spectacular with her first screen role as Jenny Lind in the 1930 film, "A Lady's Morals." In 1935 she was nominated for an Academy Award for Best Actress while under contract to Columbia Pictures for her acting and singing role in "One Night of Love." Up to her last movie, "Louise" in 1938, she had as male co-stars Carry Grant, Melvyn Douglas, Franchot Tone and many others in various films. It was mainly through her efforts that opera music became more accessible to mainstream audiences in the movies.

Blessed with a powerful but sweet soprano voice and a beautiful face she became known as "The Tennessee Nightingale."

As to her personal life, she married a Spanish movie actor, Valentin Parera in Cannes, France, in 1931. Although they had no children, the couple maintained residences in Cannes, Hollywood and Connecticut. Ironically it was in Cannes where she became involved in an international incident. In 1938 upon being introduced to the Duchess of Windsor (the former Wallis Simpson), she made the mistake of curtsying to the wife of the former King of England. (The Duchess not being a royal subject was not entitled to being greeted in that fashion).

In her typical sharp wit Grace replied, "She would have been a royal duchess long ago if she had not been an American. After all, she gave happiness and courage of his convictions to one man, which is more than most women could do. She deserves a curtsy for that alone."

Throughout her career in the 1930's she received international acclaim, receiving many awards from the King of Denmark and the French Government amongst others. Tennessee honored her by making Grace a "Tennessee Colonel" and a life member of the Tennessee State Society of Washington.

In 1944 Ms. Moore wrote and published her autobiography, *You're Only Human Once."*

On January 26th, 1947 her brilliant career abruptly ended when she was killed in an airplane crash at the Copenhagen, Denmark airport. Another notable killed in the accident was Prince Gustaf Adolf of Sweden who was second in line to the Swedish throne. He was also the father of the future King of Sweden, King Carl XVI Gustaf.

After her death in 1953, Grace Moore's life was made into a movie, "So This Is Love," starring singer Kathryn Grayson.

South Pittsburg's Silent Movie Stars

In 2004 the City of South Pittsburg dedicated a Tennessee Historical Commission plaque near the birth place of one of its most famous but relatively unknown citizens to the modern generation. November 21, 2004, was a wet and dreary day and attracted only a small crowd of 46 people to witness the unveiling of the two sided commemorative sign near the location where the renowned celebrity was born in 1899 at 324 S. Cedar Avenue.

South Pittsburg in Marion County is now better known for its annual Cornbread Festival each spring, but between 1921-1933 our celebrity became known as one of the leading ladies in the silent movie industry in California.

The beautiful and talented **Jobyna Ralston-Arlen** was born on November 21, 1899, in South Pittsburg and started acting at the age of nine in the newly opened Wilton Theatre/Opera House in her home town. At the tender age of sixteen she migrated to New York City and performed as a singer and dancer in several Broadway productions before moving to Hollywood and becoming the leading lady in six films with silent screen superstar, Harold Lloyd.

In 1927 she was featured in the first Academy Award winning film, "Wings" whose cast included Buddy Rogers, Clara Bow, Gary Cooper and her future husband, Richard Arlen. She appeared in nearly one hundred silent films and two "talkies" before she ended her acting career in 1931.

Her last movie was "Rough Waters" and her co-star was Rin Tin Tin, the famous German Shepherd. She suffered from rheumatism and several strokes and died in Los Angeles at the age of sixty-seven. She succumbed to pneumonia in 1967 while a resident at the Motion Picture County Home in Woodland Hill in Los Angeles.

Although not born in South Pittsburg, a second superstar of the silent screen era lived there from 1907-1908 before becoming a Hollywood idol. **Tom Mix** was born in Mix Run, Pennsylvania, on January 6, 1880. Unlike the relatively quiet life of Jobyna Ralston, his lifestyle was filled with more fiction than fact. A website article at www.teaxas-escapes.com by Mike Cox titled "Tom Mix: Don't Mess With the Myth" is a humorous and enlightening story about the many exaggerated tales about Mix' life.

Mix' connection to South Pittsburg is that he allegedly worked as a labor foreman at the Dixie Portland Cement Plant and as a town marshal, security guard, or alleged sheriff of Copenhagen (Richard City). In 1908 he arrived in California and was featured in his first movie, titled "The Cowboy Millionaire," on October 21, 1909.

Throughout the 1920's Mix is credited with starring in 291 movies with all but nine being silent. He was recognized as "King of the Cowboys" who reportedly made over 6 million dollars (104 million in 2015 value) during his movie career. However, Mix was an extravagant spender, loved fast cars and lived on an expensive estate. He was particularly popular with the viewing audience because he performed his own dangerous stunts and did not use a double. As a result he sustained several injuries. Almost as popular as Mix was his beautiful and intelligent spotted horse, "Tony the Wonder Horse."

Many of the tales about Mix's life were created by the publicists in the motion picture industry. The rumor that he had been a Rough Rider with Theodore Roosevelt in Santiago, Cuba, allegedly arose out of Mix riding with a group of actual Rough Riders in an annual parade in Los Angeles.

At the close of his movie career, a radio series entitled "Tom Mix Ralston Straight Shooters" went on the air in 1933 and remained a popular weekly show well into the early 1950's after Mix's death in 1940. Rumors arose that his voice was never heard on the radio because he had suffered a gunshot wound to his throat, while other versions simply stated that a variety of actors played his part on the air.

Although Mix is credited by some with helping John Wayne (Marion Morrison) get started in the motion picture industry after dropping out of the University of Southern California, Mix had few nice things to say about Wayne after the younger man became a rising star and competitor to the older performer.

On October 12, 1940, while headed to Phoenix, Arizona, Mix ran off the road in his 1937 Cord 812 Phaeton, and a heavy metal suitcase came loose and broke his neck. His funeral on October 16, 1940, was attended by thousands of adoring fans and leading personalities. He was honored posthumously with a star on the Hollywood Walk of Fame and was inducted into several Western Halls of Fame.

In the last official census held in 2010, the population of South Pittsburg, Tennessee, was listed at 2,992 citizens. Possibly no other small town in America with that number of residents has enjoyed the recognition of its connection to two of America's most popular movie stars during the 1910-1940 silent movie era.

Jobyna Ralston-Arlen

Tom Mix

Dinah Shore
Winchester & McMinnville's Movie Star

February 29, 2016, marked the 100th birthday date of Frances Rose Shore, better known as Dinah Shore, in Winchester, Tennessee.

It has been a well-kept secret that when Dinah was two years old she contacted polio. She was fortunate to recover from that deadly disease in that era, and she still sustained a deformed foot and limp.

When she was eight years old, the Shore family moved to McMinnville, Tennessee, where her father opened a Jewish department store. While she was still in grammar school, the family relocated to Nashville where she attended Hume-Fogg High School and later graduated from Vanderbilt University with a degree in sociology in 1938.

It was in Nashville that she got her musical start by singing on the WSM-AM radio station. During her studies at Vanderbilt she went to New York City to audition for positions on other radio stations and orchestras. She was initially rejected in her attempts to secure employment as a singer by the Dorsey Brothers (Jimmy and Tommy) and Benny Goodman during the Big Band era.

Her singing career was most successful in the 1940-1950's. She had ninety-one hit recordings between 1940 and 1974.

With the advent of television, new venues opened up for Dinah. In 1949-1950, she made many guest appearances on shows headed by Bob Hope, Ed Wynn and others.

Eddie Cantor became one of her supporters. He signed her as a performer on his radio show, "Time to Smile" in 1940. Dinah gave him great credit for helping her to develop her stage talents and to encourage strong fan support. During this time she recorded her first hit record "Yes, My Darling Daughter" which sold over 500,000 copies over a short period of time.

Her first personal program, "The Dinah Shore Show" first aired on November 27, 1951. She won several Emmy awards for said show which introduced her future theme song "See the USA in Your Chevrolet."

Her career further took off in 1943 when she started her first radio show, "Call to Music," and she also appeared in her first movie with

Eddie Cantor, "Thank Your Lucky Stars." During World War II she was a favorite with the troops and regularly appeared at USO shows in the states and overseas in Europe, along with numerous musicians and Hollywood performers. Prior to his untimely death in a plane crash, band leader Glen Miller performed jointly with Dinah.

In 1943 she met actor George Montgomery who would become her first husband on December 3, 1943. The union of the two produced a daughter, Melissa Ann Montgomery, in 1948, and they also adopted a son, John David Montgomery, in 1954.

Numerous hit records were produced in the 1950's until her last top twenty chart number "*Chantez, Chantez*" was recorded at RCA studios in 1957. Although her recording career began to decline, she maintained a forty-year career in television with specials and variety shows and a couple of talk show.

When "TV Guide" prepared a list of the top fifty television stars, Dinah was selected as number 16.

In 1974 she was awarded an Emmy but received notification of the cancellation of her television series, "Dinah's Place," the same day,

In spite of her Southern draw and her ladylike manner, Dinah had many romantic relationships with fellow actors Jimmy Stewart, Wayne Rogers, Dean Martin, "Tarzan" actor Ron Ely, Rod Taylor and musicians Frank Sinatra, Gene Krupa, Andy Williams, Eddie Fisher and others.

During the 1970's, she was involved in a spring-to-fall romance with young actor Burt Reynolds who was twenty years her junior. It was a highly public romance that benefited both of their images and careers.

Throughout her career, she won a Peabody Award, a Golden Globe, and a total of nine Emmy's in the entertainment fields. From 1943-1980 she appeared in fifteen motion pictures and was awarded stars on the Hollywood Walk of Fame at three different locations.

An avid supporter of women's professional golf, she was instrumental in bringing about a greater public awareness of female participation in the sport. She helped found the Colgate Dinah Shore golf tournament on the LPGA tour. She was selected as an honorary member of the LPGA Hall of Fame in 1994 and the World Golf Hall of Fame in 1998.

She died on February 24, 1994, after being diagnosed with ovarian cancer in 1993, and was cremated.

Her memory lives on through her daughter, Melissa Montgomery, who owns most of the rights to her television series. They are periodically showed as specials with special guests who are mostly deceased.

Her original hometown, Winchester, has named a public street Dinah Shore Boulevard in her memory. The Old Jail Museum at number 400 on the street in downtown contains memorabilia previously owned by her.

Burt Reynolds and Dinah Shore

Peggy Dow
Athens, Tennessee, Movie Star

While the names of Jane Russell and Marilyn Monroe may be more familiar to the viewing public of the motion picture industry, in the early 1950's the name of Peggy Dow was familiar as a prominent actress in that era. More importantly she was a resident of Athens, Tennessee, during a portion of her early years.

Although Peggy only made nine movies, like Grace Kelly who gave up her career to marry Prince Rainier of Monaco, she retired from being an actress to marry Tulsa, Oklahoma, oil man, Walter Helmerich, before he became prominent.

Peggy Dow was born Margaret Varnadow on March 18, 1928, in Columbus, Mississippi. At age four her family moved to Covington, Louisiana. They would later move to Athens, Tennessee.

She would attend a high school called Gulf Park College for Women in Gulf Port, Mississippi, and college at Northwestern University in Evanston, Illinois, where she studied for her acting career.

Several future stars on the stage and screen were also at Northwestern while Peggy was a student. The most memorable one in her class was a future comedian, Paul Lynde. Charlton Heston, Patricia Neal and Clovis Leachman were students at the university a couple of years before Peggy. During her senior year she went to California to visit a classmate whose father had died, and her acting career began.

In Hollywood she obtained an agent and signed a contract with Universal International. She attended an in-studio class of young actors including Tony Curtis and Piper Laurie.

For two years, Peggy lived at the Hollywood Studio Club, which was a women's hotel that was sponsored by Mr. Cecil B. DeMille. Marilyn Monroe was one of the other girls residing there.

Her first public acting role took place in a television show in 1949 titled "Your Show Time" in a segment titled "The Mummy's Foot."

She was under an exclusive seven-year contract that would not allow her to work for any other studio without Universal's permission.

She made her film debut in "Woman in Hiding" (1950) with Ida Lupino in the title role along with Stephen McNally.

The second of the nine movies in her abbreviated movie career between 1949-1951 was "Undertow" filmed in Chicago. Her third film was "The Sleeping City" (1950) which starred Richard Conte as a detective in New York City. She was invited to an opening party given by the cast of "Gentlemen Prefer Blonds," and it was there she met Walter Helmerich who would later become her husband and father of their five sons. What would follow would be a whirlwind romance with Walter which resulted in marriage after nine movies and ended a prominent movie career.

Before she retired from acting to become the wife of Walter Helmerich who would become a millionaire in the oil business and philanthropist in the Tulsa area, she performed in "Shakedown" in 1950 which co-starred Brian Donlevy and Howard Duff.

"The Sleeping City" (1950) followed as one of the first films to be shot exclusively at one location – Bellevue Hospital in New York. It starred Richard Conte in a murder thriller.

She had her first role in a famous movie with Jimmy Stewart in the classic "Harvey" where she played the role of the nurse. She spoke glowingly of Jimmy Stewart as she did with all of her leading men.

Another memorable movie was "Bright Victory" with Arthur Kennedy who portrayed a blind veteran that won him an Oscar for Best Actor in 1951.

Her last three movies in 1951 before retiring to domestic life as a wife and mother were "I Want You" and two family films, "Reunion in Reno" and "You Never Can Tell."

She was also chosen to present an Oscar to Edith Head at the Academy Awards in 1950 for dress designing, and three of the movies she performed in 1950-1951 in were nominated for Academy Awards. She was listed among the top four cast members each time.

On a trip back to Athens for Christmas, she agreed to meet Walt Helmerich at the airport in Tulsa for a thirty minute layover for a Coca-Cola. When the aircraft had to be repaired for a delay of four-five hours, he gave Peggy a tour of Tulsa which was more of a cosmopolitan community than she realized.

He eventually talked her into marrying him when he escorted her to Washington to receive an award from President Harry Truman for the film "Bright Victory" on the condition that she would marry him.

They were married on November 23, 1951, in Athens and were leaders and philanthropists in the Tulsa area until his death in 2012. Her last invitation to perform in the movies was from renowned actor William Holden after the birth of her first son. She was invited to be the leading actress in the "Bridges of Toko-Ri," which ironically was played by Grace Kelly.

Peggy Dow Helmrich, *Tulsa World*, November, 30, 2015 photo by James Gibbard

Although very little is written in the news media about her life in Athens, she is another Hollywood movie star with contacts to the Volunteer State. She still resides in Tulsa and remains active in her nineties as a strong supporter of the arts and libraries.

In 2019, the Women for OSU (Oklahoma State University) honored her as the 2019 Philanthropist of the Year on April the twenty-fifth.

Nellie Kenyon
Chattanooga News Reporter Extraordinaire

In the history of journalism in the Chattanooga area a slight woman with an inquisitive sense of news reporting stands at the top of the list of talented reporters who covered the important events and court cases in the early twentieth century.

Nellie Kenyon was born in 1898 and was the daughter of a society and club editor for the *Chattanooga News* which later would become the *Chattanooga Times*, flagship of the *New York Times* owned by the Adolph Ochs family.

As a young high school student, she developed the reputation of a tough newspaper reporter in the male dominated profession.

She was assigned to the historic Scopes "Monkey" trial in Dayton, Tennessee in 1925. She met famous newspaper writer H.L. Mencken of the *Baltimore Sun* who was covering the trial for his paper. When Mencken asked Nellie what were the social opportunities on a Saturday night in the rural community she informed him that there were only three options; 1.) attend the only movie theater in Dayton; 2.) watch the monkeys brought into town by Barnum and Bailey Circus as part of the public spectacle; or 3.) attend a service at a "Holy Roller Church." Expressing ignorance of such church activities he agreed to accompany Nellie to observe what transpired at said meeting, and then he wrote a column as part of his continuous criticism of the events occurring in Rhea County thirty miles north of Chattanooga.

After Al "Scarface" Capone was convicted of income tax evasion in Chicago in 1932, he was traveling by train to the federal prison in Atlanta to begin serving his sentence prior to eventually being transported to Alcatraz to finish the balance. Using her persuasive and aggressive talents she was able to get an interview on the train with America's most notorious criminal of the era. According to legend, Nellie asked Capone, "Who is going to manage the store while you are gone?" Big Al is supposed to have flippantly said, "You are, Cutie!"

Through the use of her investigative instincts, Nellie was able to help the police capture the robber who had held up the Highland Park

Bank in Chattanooga. The case was solved by Nellie showing the investigating officers how their main suspect had planned the crime by following the same pattern of conduct outlined in some detective magazine he had left in his boarding house, along with a handcuff key that matched the one used to shackle the bank tellers.

She moved to Nashville in 1940 to work for the *Nashville Tennessean* where she covered state government and the federal courts until she retired in 1970.

Her philosophy about being a reporter was; 1.) keep the story simple; 2.) don't take sides; and 3.) be fiery in your investigation and writing of the story.

In describing her work ethics, she stated that she was told, "If there was a Pulitzer Prize for persistence – I'd get it."

In 1982 she died in a nursing home in Nashville and is buried at Forrest Hills Cemetery in St. Elmo.

She was a pioneer in opening up the field of investigative reporting for women in Tennessee in journalism!

Nellie Kenyon, back to camera, covering the Scopes Trial in 1925

Nellie Kenyon making notes alongside Jimmy Hofa, March 14, 1964, during his trial in Chattanooga. Photos courtesy the *Tennesseean*

Drue Smith
Woman Pioneer In Journalism And Media

One of the many mysteries surrounding the long, illustrious and sometimes unorthodox career of Drue Smith in the journalism, broadcasting and political histories of Tennessee, was her ability to conceal her birth date.

Born in Chattanooga, the date believed to have been in the era surrounding World War I, she lived a colorful lifetime of outstanding service to her community in both her hometown and the state capitol of Nashville.

While a student at Girls Preparatory School (GPS) in Chattanooga, she became interested in journalism. She started her career as a female reporter during the early entry of women into the newspaper industry. She was given an opportunity by both Adolph Ochs, head of the *Chattanooga Times*, and Roy McDonald, founder of the *Chattanooga News-Free Press*. She wrote as a society editor for the *Times*, but it would not be long before she expanded her influence into the broadcasting arenas of radio and television.

Chattanooga's second radio station, WAPO (now WGOW), founded in 1936, hired her as a commentator. She is credited with giving Congressman Estes Kefauver the coonskin cap which he successfully used in his senate race in 1948 against Senator Kenneth McKellar and the Crump political machine in Shelby County.

When WDEF-TV became Chattanooga's first television station in 1954. Drue went on the air with her own show, "Drue's Party Line," which covered local events. A written version was circulated through several newspapers.

Summoned to Nashville by Governor Frank G. Clement, she served as information liaison for the news media during his administration. She became a contributor to all three major national television networks and later became the first woman to cover the Tennessee General Assembly on a full-time basis. She also served as the first woman to serve as the head of the Capitol Hill Press Corps.

As a reward for an outstanding career and service the legislature named the Capitol Press Room in her behalf. Always outspoken and colorful, she was known for her bright hats and zany outfits. She drove a flashy red Mustang automobile that was covered with bumper stickers for politicians of both parties, and quipped that she drove slowly, "So everyone can read them all."

However, she earned the respect of politicians in both political parties and was publicly admired by Governor Winfield Dunn, Lamar Alexander, Ned McWherter, and Phil Bredesen, as well as other political leaders. She also has often been credited with discovering Oprah Winfrey when Drue covered a beauty contest where Oprah was competing for the title of "Miss Fire Prevention." She also was close friends with country singer Eddie Arnold, actor Jim Neighbors, actress June Allyson, comedienne Minnie Pearl, and many others.

Being appointed an honorary member of the Tennessee National Guard, she was able to fly on military aircrafts and report on the summer camps activities of the part-time soldiers.

In 1962 President John F. Kennedy designated her to represent Tennessee on the Defense Advisory Committee for Women in the Services.

She achieved several other firsts for women in her chosen field, including the 1984 joint resolution by the Tennessee General Assembly appointing her as the honorary 133rd member of that body.

The Middle Tennessee Chapter of the Society of Professional Journalist's selected Drue as its first female member and president. As further recognition of valuable service to the association, in 1997 the body named their journalism scholarship after her.

In 1989 the Tennessee Association of Broadcasters gave her a lifetime membership in honor of her stellar lifetime service as a member of the broadcasting industry. Many other organizations honored her for outstanding service on behalf of women. These included the American Women in Radio and Television, Tennessee Press Women, Altrusa Club, and the Pilot Club.

When she died late in February 2001, she was buried at the Chattanooga Memorial Park at White Oak outside Chattanooga in a very simple ceremony, contrary to the colorful life that exemplified her as one of the pioneer women in the field of journalism and broadcasting. The unsolved mystery of her date of birth continued and was not revealed at her burial.

Former Hamilton County State Representative, Brenda Turner, gave a eulogy and stated, "There are not many words to describe Drue in the dictionary that you would leave out," and "That everyone whose lives she touched had a story about her – or three of four."

Her daughter, Drucilla Fuller, prepared a biography *Drue Smith's Amazing Technicolor Dream Life* in 2005 which covers her over sixty- year career in the broadcasting and print media. The publication features 139 photographs that depict her career in the newspaper and radio and television industries. The book is also part of the Drue Smith exhibit, 20th Century Collection, Tennessee State Museum, 505 Deadrick Street, Nashville, Tennessee 37243.

Cover of Drucilla Fuller's book, *Drue Smith's Amazing Technicolor Dream Life.*

Space in this article is inadequate to fully describe the impact of this interesting and pioneer woman in Chattanooga and the state. Her unique and often outrageous outfits failed to demonstrate the significant contributions she made in protecting the First Amendment Rights of the citizens of the state.

As a final recognition of her career, the Tennessee Journalism Hall of Fame posthumously inducted her into its body on August 11, 2015, in Murfreesboro, along with one of her early benefactors, Roy McDonald of the *Chattanooga News-Free Press.*

Ralph E. McGill
Soddy's Civil Rights Advocate

Ralph Emerson McGill was born on a farm outside Soddy, Tennessee, on February 5, 1898. It was unusual for students from that venue to attend the prestigious McCallie School for boys during this era which was also segregated.

As a result of his prep school education at McCallie he was able to gain admittance to Vanderbilt University in Nashville.

His career was interrupted by a tour of duty in the United State Marine Corps in World War I, but he returned to Vanderbilt and almost graduated as a senior, but he was suspended from the institution for writing an article in the university's student newspaper that was critical of the school administration. Evidently he never received a diploma from that university or elsewhere.

During 1922-1923 McGill worked for the now defunct *Nashville Banner* as a rookie sportswriter. He would gradually become the sports editor of the newspaper. During his employment with the *Banner*, McGill would sometimes write articles on sports subjects for the *Atlanta Constitution* in Georgia.

In 1931 he accepted a position with that paper to become its sports editor. During that time frame through 1938, he also wrote many non-sports articles which led McGill to be hired as executive editor in 1939 by Clark Howell, editor the *Constitution* to write on both sports and politics.

Due to their popularity, he would have three columns in the paper as the leading articles in the sports section ("Break Days"), editorial page ("One Word More"), and a feature on the front page entitled ("Ralph McGill".)

He later served as editor of the paper from 1942-1960 and was eventually elevated to publisher from 1960 until his death in 1969. During the controversial 1960's, McGill was described as, "A voice of moderation in the South," on the explosive subject of segregation versus integration.

His courage in publicizing public corruption and racial inequality resulted in his becoming both loved and hated by many.

His stands resulted in angry letters and death threats being sent to McGill and the *Constitution* paper. The inevitable cross burning on the lawn of his home, gunfire into his house, and the placing of bombs in his mailbox were the results of McGill's courageous stands against the Ku Klux Klan and opposition to segregation.

He courageously took on segregationist Georgia Governor, Herman Talmadge, in his editorials in addition to the Klan. McGill also won a Rosenwald Fellowship during the late 1950's, which had allowed him to travel throughout Europe and to personally view the Nazi takeover of Austria in 1938.

His enlightened editorial campaign during this turbulent era resulted in his being awarded a Pulitzer Prize in 1958.

McGill's advocacy in support of full civil rights for African Americans throughout the country earned him a Presidential Medal of Freedom in 1964 from President Lyndon B. Johnson. He also became a friend of President John F. Kennedy, often serving as a civil rights advocate.

McGill retained his popularity with a large segment of the Southern populace because he advocated moderation and never completely pushed for integration in his columns but urged cooperation between the races and compliance with federal law on the subject. Another theory as to his moderate position was a legitimate concern that the paper would lose many of its subscribers and readers if it took a strong stand opposing segregation in this era.

He was a vociferous traveler and personally observed what was happening in Europe as Hitler rose to power in Germany.

Following World War II, he traveled and wrote stories on Africa, Russia, the far East and our military deployment in Vietnam. Democratic presidents Truman, Kennedy, and Johnson and Republican president Eisenhower sought his input as to what he observed on his world travels.

He also wrote a popular book, *The South and the Southerner*, in 1963 that won an award from "The Atlantic" magazine as an outstanding non-fiction publication.

He was respected by African-Americans and was described by Dr. Martin Luther King, Jr. in his treatise of April, 1963, "Letter from the Birmingham Jail" as being "one of the few enlightened white persons" to understand and agree with the civil rights movement.

Numerous members of the McGill family still reside in the Soddy Daisy area. Whether Ralph McGill's progressive viewpoints expressed in *The Atlantic Constitution* during the 1950-1960's era were in agreement with those of his local relatives would be a matter of conjecture.

However, he was asked to address the Soddy Daisy High School commencement in his later years. On returning home he found that everything had changed since his youth. He recalled for the students the "unpainted general store that smelled of tobacco, calico, and dry goods, of cheese, kerosene and bananas."

McGill died of a heart attack on February 3, 1969, two days before his 71st birthday.

Ralph Emerson McGill. Photo courtesy Chattanooga Times Free-Press.

John N. Popham, III
Chattanooga's Iconic Newsman

The history of newspaper reporting in Chattanooga has included many talented journalists. None have been more influential and colorful than John Popham who served as news editor of the *Chattanooga Times* from 1958 until his retirement in 1977.

Upon his death on December 12th, 1999, state and national newspapers collectively described him as, "A descendant of European pilgrims to America, the Virginia gentleman from the house of Popham, the World War II decorated Marine, the cub reporter in Brooklyn, New York in 1930, the United Nations correspondent, the first *New York Times* Southern correspondent, a beloved husband and father, the dutiful but not uncritical Catholic, the legendary managing editor of the *Chattanooga Times*."

However there is so much more that could be written about this literary giant's life, in not only Chattanooga but the entire South and nation.

Three colorful and controversial mayors of New York City, William Dwyer, James Walker, and Forello LaGuardia, all asked him to be director of public relations for the Municipality, which he refused.

During the turbulent era of development of civil rights from 1947-1958, he covered that period for the *New York Times* by traveling all over the South to investigate the turmoil taking place following the end of World War II and the United States Supreme Court decisions outlawing segregation in 1954.

"Pop" or "Johnny" became a traveling vagabond in fifteen states throughout the South with the unique ability to make friends on both sides of the controversial issue of segregation. It was common for him to be on the road fifty thousand miles a year covering the South in both urban and rural communities.

Traveling alone, he covered the stories of how the South was changing after the end of the war and legal banishment of the controversy over the separation of the races. His journeys were not without personal risk or danger. Pop was jailed in Jackson, Mississippi, based on his diligent inquiry into the racial strife of the times and was released upon orders of the governor of the state.

During the racial problems at Clinton, Tennessee, he was shot at, and his coverage of the changing South placed him in numerous dangerous situations. However, his ability to listen to both sides of the controversial issue gave him a credibility that also gave him the opportunity and standing to be a mentor to reporters from outside the South who covered crisis's like the forced integration of Little Rock Central High School in Arkansas.

He developed his stories not only by talking to politicians and public officials, but also by visiting with and gaining confidence of citizens with his warmth and southern charm.

Chattanoogan Ruth Holmberg, who was publisher of the *Chattanooga Times*, recalled "Pop" as an, "Almost Damon Runyon caricature of a newsman with a deep Southern accent and fast delivery."

Popham's successor as the *New York Times* Southern correspondent in Atlanta, Claude F. Sitton described his speech delivery as, "Dollops of sorghum syrup from a Gatling gun."

When he became a reporter and later managing editor of the *Chattanooga Times,* the paper became the informal center of the national coverage of the Civil Rights movement.

For twenty-two years after his retirement, "Pop" observed with dismay his perceived demise of the free standing *Chattanooga Times*, and the ultimate merger with the paper's longtime political rival since the 1930's, the Republican oriented *Chattanooga News-Free Press*.

The merge of the two papers in January, 1999, was upsetting to Popham, and he permanently terminated his relationship with the paper where he had still worked on a part time basis and wrote an occasional article. However his interest in the law never waned, and at the age of seventy-two in 1985, he completed a five year odyssey and received his law degree from John Marshall Law School in Atlanta after commuting from Chattanooga.

Never intending to officially enter the practice of law, he however combined his new legal knowledge and his lifetime military and journalism history backgrounds to become an entertaining source of knowledge amongst his old friends and newspaper associates (and lawyers) who were privileged to be in his company prior to his death in 1999 at the age of eighty-nine.

The lively afternoon exchanges on all topics between "Pop," Bill Casteel, Nathan Crowe, Flop Fuller and many others in Chattanooga's less than five-star dining establishments unfortunately were never recorded for historical posterity.

John Popham, III, was the perfect prototype for investigative reporters during his entire life and particularly the turbulent Civil Rights Era.

John Popham courtesy of the
Atlanta Journal and Constitution

Charles Bartlett
Pulitzer Prize Reporter and Matchmaker

Chattanooga has a rich and impressive history of providing Pulitzer Prize winners to the literary world.

Former Soddy resident and McCallie graduate, Ralph McGill, of the *Atlanta Constitution* in 1958; 1959 Baylor School graduate, Wendell Rawls; photographer, Robin Hood, in 1977; investigative reporter, Bill Dedman, in 1989; and another McCallie and Sewanee graduate, Jon Meachem, have all won this prestigious award in different categories.

However the first Pulitzer Prize award winner in 1956, Charles Bartlett, is one of the most diverse and interesting individuals in this selective group. He also had tremendous influence with an American president.

Bartlett was born on August 14, 1921, in Chicago, Illinois, to a prominent and wealthy family which allowed him to attend and graduate from Yale University obtaining a degree in journalism in 1943.

He entered the Navy as an intelligence officer in the Pacific during World War II. During that tour of duty he became acquainted with another young Navy Officer, John F. Kennedy, of Boston, Massachusetts. This relationship would continue to grow until Kennedy's death in 1963 in Dallas, Texas. Bartlett's contacts with the Kennedy family would exist until his death on February 17, 2017, at his Washington, D.C. home.

His family were social acquaintances with members of the Sulzberger publishing dynasty. This relationship led him to obtain a position as a reporter at the flagship paper of the *New York Times* in Chattanooga and move to Lookout Mountain outside Chattanooga.

While working at the *Chattanooga Times* he won a Pulitzer Prize in 1956 for a series of articles that led to a Senate investigation into a conflict of interest charge involving Harold E. Talbott, the secretary of the Air Force in President Eisenhower's administration.

Despite some reluctance to pursue the investigation of Talbott because of his popularity, Bartlett obtained the support of Robert Kennedy who was serving as legal counsel on the Senate's Homeland Security and Governmental Affairs Subcommittee on investigations. It was Kennedy's aggressive persistence at the committee hearings which eventually led to Talbott's resignation from his position in August 1955.

A revelation that Talbott had steered government contracts to a company in which he had financial interest was the basis for his resignation.

Due to his family's social position and residence in Palm Beach, Florida, Bartlett first met John F. Kennedy at a local night club called Ta-Boo. Out of that initial meeting would develop a lifelong political and social relationship.

Bartlett had briefly dated Jacqueline Bouvier but reports are that she "found him too buttoned-down for her taste." As a result he became a matchmaker by arranging a blind date between the two future spouses. Some sources contend that Bartlett was urged by the patriarch of the Kennedy family, Joe Kennedy, to find an acceptable mate for Jack to benefit his political career.

Bartlett assumed the role of matchmaker and the couple married in September 1953, just two years after being introduced at a dinner party at the Bartlett's home in Georgetown. The Bartletts were part of the wedding party in Newport, Rhode Island. They also would be present for the baptism of the Kennedy's infant son, John Jr.

Bartlett, who had joined the *Chattanooga Times* in 1946, became its Washington correspondent in 1948. He would continue in that capacity until he moved to the *Chicago Sun Times* in 1963.

He was a close confidant to President Kennedy and regularly advised him on crucial issues during Jack's term of office.

As a reporter and insider with President Kennedy, Bartlett had to walk a tight rope to avoid compromising both positions. He was quoted as saying, "It was not possible to be a good newsman and be a close friend of the president," admitting his desire to help Kennedy succeed as president.

He co-authored an article with journalists Stewart Alsop in the "Saturday Evening Post" on the 1962 Cuban missile crisis that introduced the use of the phrases "hawks and doves" and "eyeball to eyeball." The story resulted in a controversy over the role of Adali Stevenson, II, who was the United States Ambassador to the United Nations. Stevenson was depicted as an appeaser willing to take the Guantanamo military base out of service in return for the Soviets removing their missiles from Cuba.

Other authors described Bartlett as a self-seeking informal counsel. He became known as the sender of memos to the president which JFK called "Bartlettisms" on a variety of subjects that ranged from foreign policy matter to treatment of the president's bad back.

In later years Bartlett was interviewed many times about his relationship with Jack Kennedy. He described Kennedy as a very complex individual who would engage a person in conversation on his own initiative, and question for information, but always kept a distance from the interviewer.

It was the mystique and Kennedy's ability to compartmentalize everything that created an aura where everyone only saw parts of his personality.

In one interview Bartlett told the questioner, "No one even knew John Kennedy....not all of him."

Bartlett also co-authored the book *Facing the Brink: An Intimate Study of Crisis Diplomacy* (1967) with former journalist Edward Weintal.

John and Jackie Kennedy on their wedding day

Anna Mae Clift
The Soddy Girl and the Memphis Belle

The legendary World War II B-17 bomber, the Memphis Belle, has a strong connection to the north Hamilton County community of Soddy in the City of Soddy Daisy.

Anna Mae Clift, descendant of the pioneer Clift family, was born on October 26, 1896, but not in Soddy. It is believed her birthplace was either Chattanooga or Birmingham, Alabama. Descendants of the Clift family still proudly claim their heritage in the Soddy Daisy area. At an early age, around 1916, the tall red-headed beauty, Anna Mae, migrated to New York City (NYC) to become a dancer with the Ziegfeld Follies on Broadway in the heart of the theater district.

One day she was spied by a young Peruvian artist, Alberto Vargas, who was captivated by her beauty and charm. Normally a very shy individual, he followed her to a local theater where she was in the chorus line, and he asked a doorman for her name.

Vargas waited several hours until she came out of the theater and then approached her. He asked to be allowed to paint her portrait but said that he had no money to pay her. Surprisingly she agreed to pose for him, and what followed was a storybook romance that did not even end with her death in 1974.

Vargas fell in love with Anna Mae immediately but was too timid to reveal his true feelings. Initially they became close friends, and she became the prototype for all of the watercolors that he drew up until his death in 1982.

Because Anna Mae was a beautiful showgirl, somewhat of a gadfly, and who loved to party, Alberto was reluctant to express his true feelings of love because he was afraid she would reject him and terminate their relationship. Unbeknownst to him, Anna Mae felt the same about him, and in 1930 she proposed the idea of marriage which he immediately accepted.

Vargas' career included several categories. He first found work retouching negatives for a photographer. Later he became a freelance artist selling pen-and-ink drawings.

In 1919, Florenz Ziegfeld, head of the Ziegfeld Follies, hired him full time to paint promotional portraits of his Ziegfeld girls including Anna Mae. Vargas became their official portrait painter, and he and Ziegfeld achieved success with each other for twelve years on a verbal contract sealed by a handshake.

In 1934, Twentieth Century Fox brought Anna Mae and Alberto to Hollywood where he painted most of the leading ladies of that day including Greta Garbo, Dorothy Lamour, Barbara Stanwyck, Marlene Dedrick, and child star, Shirley Temple, amongst others.

Being a handsome Latin male one might think that he would be tempted by all of the beautiful women in Hollywood to stray from his marriage vows. Such was not the case as he remained true to his only love besides art, Anna Mae.

In 1939 Vargas supported a labor strike which resulted in his being terminated and blacklisted in the motion picture industry.

In May 1940, he traveled to Manhattan hoping to find employment to get him out of his financial difficulties. He secured a job with "Esquire" magazine where he replaced another artist named George Petty, who had created a scantily clad pin-up girl known as The Petty Girl.

An argument with 'Esquire's" owner – publisher George Sharp, resulted in Petty being fired and replaced by Alberto Vargas. Vargas made the mistake of accepting the job on another handshake deal. This would result in many lawsuits and legal battles over who was the owner of the Vargas paintings and trademarks that were drawn while Alberto was at "Esquire."

In 1953 he met a young adman named Hugh Hefner, who became the creator of "Playboy" magazine. Alberto would publish 152 paintings of lovely young women over sixteen years as part of a regular feature of the magazine. His works became known as the "Varga Girls" and Alberto was heralded as the "The King of Pin-up Art" during the liberated 1960's.

A naturalized and patriotic American during World War II, Alberto Vargas and his Varga Girl became a morale-building part of the war effort. The prototype of Anna Mae was actually drawn by George Petty, but it was built on one of the drawings of Alberto's with minor changes. The images appeared on posters promoting patriotism and the

A Varga Girl, modeled after Anna Mae Clift, was painted on the Memphis Belle

purchase of war bonds, and her image appeared on the backs of pilots' leather jackets.

Most importantly it was on both sides of the B-17 bomber, "The Memphis Belle" which has been immortalized in verse and on the silver screen in two full length movies in 1941 and 1990. The plane successfully completed the required twenty-five missions and is credited with eight kills of German fighters. Each of the ten member crew were awarded the Distinguished Flying Cross and the Air Medal.

Anna Mae and Alberto lived a complex and unhappy life, but their love affair endured until she died from a fall in their Westwood, California, bungalow that they had bought in 1936. Heartbroken and depressed, Alberto never recovered from her death and finally died in 1982 at the age of 86.

When he replied to correspondence after Anna Mae's death, he would send thank you notes and would always add, "And Anna Mae sends her love too."

According to former Hamilton County Commissioner, Fred Skillern, he recalls the Vargas' spending a couple of weeks each summer for about five years in the 1960's at his father's Colonial Motel across from Soddy Lake.

The idealistic love story of the country girl with connections to Soddy and the Peruvian artist is described in greater detail in a lengthy article by Paul Chutkow entitled "The Real Vargas" in "Cigar Aficionado Magazine" in August 1996, and in numerous other articles attainable by googling Alberto Vargas or Anna Mae Clift.

The Soddy Daisy – Montlake Historical Society under President Steve Smith at slsmith01@comcast.net can provide additional information on Anna Mae Clift.

Martin W. Littleton
Rags to Riches Lawyer

Although his legal fame was acquired outside Tennessee, Martin W. Littleton (1872-1934) was born January 12, 1872, near Kingston, Tennessee, as one of nineteen children in a one-room cabin.

He never attended any school and was self-taught by his father and older sister who used a Bible and a few other books they had acquired as teaching tools.

Up to the age of eight he worked on the family farm when they moved to Weatherford, Texas. He became interested in law at this early age and attended trials at the Parker County Courthouse. Beginning at the age of eleven, he engaged in a variety of menial jobs in hopes of earning enough money to further his education. While working on the road he met the county prosecutor who offered him a job as a law clerk and janitor at the courthouse. It was in this capacity that he was able to watch trials and continue to study to be a lawyer. At the age of twenty he passed the bar in 1891.

From this humble beginning he would eventually become one of the wealthiest attorneys in the country.

In 1922 Merle Crowell authored *The Amazing Story of Martin W. Littleton* which described the attorney's life and listed him as a rags to riches success story in motivational books and articles.

He rotated between being a prosecutor and defense counsel in Parker County and eventually became a prosecutor in Dallas.

In 1896 Littleton and new bride, Maud, moved to New York City where he got a job with a law firm, but he become dissatisfied with the work. He began representing indigent defendants and quickly developed a reputation of being an excellent criminal defense lawyer.

As a fine speaker, he naturally became involved in Democratic politics. His political career including making the nomination speech for Alton B. Parker at the 1904 Democratic Convention when Barker was chosen to be the party's presidential candidate but who would eventually lose to Theodore Roosevelt.

In 1910 Littleton was elected to Congress and served one term from 1911-1913. He was narrowly defeated in a race for the U.S. Senate and wound up losing in a three-way deadlock after incurring the opposition of the Tammany Hall political machine.

In 1908, after millionaire Harry Thaw's first trial for the murder of prominent architect Sanford White on the roof top garden of the Madison Square Garden ended in a hung jury, Littleton was hired for the retrial in the first "Trial of the Century".

Littleton raised the defense of "not guilty by reason of insanity" and successfully acquitted the defendant of the criminal charge. The court committed Thaw to a mental hospital. This victory in a sensational trial spring boarded Littleton's legal career to international fame.

Producer-director D. W. Griffith's controversial film "The Birth of a Nation," led to charges being raised against Griffith in New York and in a Congressional Committee on Education. Littleton defended him successfully at the hearing in the face of opposition by the NAACP and other groups wanting censorship of the film.

His third high profile case was in the Teapot Dome scandal in the oil industry in 1928 in Wyoming. Industrialist Harry Ford Sinclair was charged with bribing United States Secretary Albert F. Fall to grant Sinclair Oil leases on government land without competitive bidding. Although Sinclair served nine months on contempt of Congress and jury tampering charges, he was acquitted of the bribery charges. "Time" magazine likened Littleton's legal maneuvering to Houdini.

Martin's wife, Maud, was instrumental in starting the campaign to preserve Thomas Jefferson's home Monticello, which ultimately was purchased in 1923 by the Thomas Jefferson Foundation, a private non-profit organization. Maud was referred to in the Hearst newspaper Syndicate as "The Lady of Monticello".

It is unfortunate that Littleton's migration to Texas at the age of eight deprived Tennessee of claiming him as one of the most prominent attorney's in history.

Judge Sue K. Hicks
"A Boy Named Sue"

Chattanooga's neighbor to the north, Rhea County, has become famous (or infamous) in American legal circles as a result of the John T. Scopes trial in 1925 on the issue of the prohibition of the theory of evolution of man from lower animals being taught in school and universities under the Tennessee statute (Butler Act) enacted by the Tennessee Legislature in March, 1925.

What started out to be a test case on evolution began in a conversation over coffee at a local drug store (F.E. Robinson) with the intention of bringing favorable attention to the rural town of Dayton. History has covered the important proceedings with mixed reviews as to whether Dayton's image has been enhanced or diminished over the years since the trial.

For about twenty-five years, the Gem Players of Etowah have put on a production at the Gem Theater in Etowah, Tennessee, of the play "Inherit the Wind" by Jerome Lawrence and Robert E. Lee. Later made into a movie, it is a fictionalized account of the trial held in 1925.

In the famous trial, two of the originators of the idea to test the constitutionality of the Butler Act by teacher John Scopes was attorney Sue K. Hicks and his brother, attorney Herbert Hicks. The roles of the two prosecutors in the legal proceedings were greatly diminished when former presidential candidate, William Jennings Bryan, and renowned criminal defense lawyer, Clarence Darrow, were employed to represent the State and the defense respectively.

The trial lasted ten days and Dayton was depicted as a backward community by the news media and particularly H.L. Mencken of the *Baltimore Sun* newspaper. A carnival atmosphere was created by both sides on the issue of evolution expressing their viewpoints with written signs, preacher's sermons, and even the presence of a live ape.

Most of the expert evidence on the issue of evolution that was attempted to be introduced by the defense was excluded by Circuit Judge John Raulston. Their testimony was heard outside the presence of the jury for the purpose of making an appellate record to be reviewed by the Tennessee Supreme Court which later upheld the constitutionality of the Butler Act but dismissed the case on the technicality that the $100.00 fine imposed by Judge Raulston on John Scopes upon a finding of guilt by the jury after only nine minutes was illegal. Tennessee law required that all fines levied against a defendant in excess of $50.00 had to be set by a jury.

Although attorney Sue K. Hicks' role in the Scopes Trial was relatively small, he would obtain name recognition and notoriety in another area of his personal life.

When his mother died shortly after giving birth to her son, his father named him Sue in honor of his late wife.

Shel Silverstein, noted cartoonist, author, poet, songwriter and playwright of children's stories, who was also probably better known as the featured cartoonist for "Playboy" magazine from 1957-1970, wrote a song, "A Boy Named Sue," that was recorded by Johnny Cash. Siverstein allegedly got the idea for the tune when he attended a judicial conference in Gatlinburg, Tennessee, where he heard Judge Hicks speak on a legal topic.

Although the story in the song is not the reason for Sue Kerr Hicks inheriting that name, it has historically been repeated that the young male lawyer with the unusual first name from Dayton, Tennessee, was the model for the song. The song won a Grammy Award in 1970.

Sue Hicks served as Circuit Judge in Tennessee between 1936 and 1958 and thereafter as a senior judge.

He was very proud of the fact that he had tried over 800 murder cases as a judge but lamented, "The most publicity has been from the name Sue and the evolution case."

Johnny Cash first sang and recorded the song about Sue at a live concert at San Quentin Prison in California. It later became a big hit for Cash, and the singer sent Judge Hicks two records and photos inscribed with the inscriptions, "To Sue, How do you do?"

Hicks died on June 17, 1980, at the age of 84 and is buried in Sweetwater, Tennessee.

John R. Neal
Scopes Eccentric Lawyer

The history of the prosecution case of State of Tennessee versus John R. Scopes in 1925 for teaching the Theory of Evolution in the high school in Rhea County, Tennessee has been well documented in both fact and fiction.

The out-of-presence of the jury cross-examination of fundamentalist Christian, William Jennings Bryan, by atheist defense lawyer, Clarence Darrow, is part of legal history as depicted in the film "Inhibit the Wind" starring Spencer Tracy, Frederick March and Gene Kelly. Clarence Darrow was brought into the case by attorney John R. Neal, an eccentric lawyer, legislator, and ex-law professor at the University of Tennessee College of Law at Knoxville.

John R. Neal was born on September 17, 1876, at Rhea Springs near Dayton, Tennessee. He received an A.B. degree from the University of Tennessee in 1893 and a law degree from Vanderbilt University in 1896. Neal also received a Ph.D. in History in 1899 and would move to Denver, Colorado, and taught law at the University of Denver.

In 1906 he was elected to the Tennessee House of Representatives and in 1908 was elected to the Tennessee Senate but was defeated in the senate primary in 1910 after making enemies with Tennessee's governor and fellow Democrats.

Neal joined the faculty of the University of Tennessee College of Law at Knoxville as a part time professor and later went on staff full time in 1917. His tenure at the law school was filled with controversy with the dean of the law school and would eventually lead to the termination of Neal and six other professors from the faculty. This became known as the "Slaughter of the Ph.D.s" in 1923.

Neal's tardiness, not showing up for roll call, an unorthodox method of grading students wherein he automatically gave each a grade of 95 irrespective of their performance in class, and deviation from the designated law text books, all contributed to his removal from the faculty. One of Neal's colleagues who was also terminated, Jesse Sprowls, claimed that he was removed from the law school faculty based on his teaching the Theory of Evolution which allegedly incurred the disfavor of Dean Malcolm McDermott. Neal rose to the defense of Sprowls and became one of the fired seven instructors.

Neal's unusual hygiene habits of rarely taking a bath, sleeping in his suits, and appearing disheveled would eventually get him banned from a public cafeteria and kicked out of his hotel room because he refused to clean or allow hotel staff to sanitize his room.

When the Butler Act (prohibition of teaching evolution) passed the Tennessee Legislature in 1923, six creative Dayton residents (including John Scopes) gathered in a famous meeting at the Robinson Drug Store and decided to attempt to bring a test case attacking the Butler Act as being unconstitutional. Although history has described the Scopes Trial as primarily a religious battle between fundamentalists and agnostics, it is generally accepted that the main reason for the suit was to improve the economic climate of Dayton and Rhea County.

When Neal learned of the proposed lawsuit, he volunteered his services and later got the famous trial lawyer Clarence Darrow to join the defense team to attack the evolution statute. An ACLU attorney and others were added as co-counsel.

When Darrow arrived in Dayton, he and Neal quickly had a difference of opinion as to trial strategy. Neal, who was still angry over his firing at the University of Tennessee, wanted to try the case as a defense of the rights of teachers, while Darrow wanted the trial to be an indictment of religious intolerance. Both attempted to get the other kicked off the case but would eventually agree to try the case together.

The trial lasted eight days, but very little actual testimony was presented to the jury. Two young students testified about the teaching of evolution by Scopes, but Scopes may not have actually taught the subject as he was primarily the coach of the athletics teams and was only substituting for the religious teacher who was on vacation. Both students would later admit that Scopes had coached them on how to testify against him.

Scopes had volunteered to be the defendant to test the evolution theory, and the carnival show began which resulted in national and international coverage. This included the first radio broadcasting of a national trial by WGN in Chicago.

Neal's role in the trial primarily consisted in his filing and arguing a motion to quash (dismiss) the indictment as being unconstitutional. Scopes was found guilty in nine minutes, as Darrow had urged the jury to find the young man guilty in order that the case could be appealed to the Tennessee Supreme Court and United States Supreme Court.

The jury had found Scopes guilty but assessed no fine. The trial judge, John T. Raulston, assessed one in the amount of $100.00 which violated the Tennessee constitutional provision that "all fines in excess of $50.00 had to be set by a jury."

Neal was given the responsibility of preparing the appeal to the Tennessee Supreme Court, but he missed the deadline to file the transcript and record of the trial, which ultimately would result in the case being dismissed on that technicality. No appeal was therefore available in the United States Supreme Court. Nevertheless, Neal attempted several times unsuccessfully to file the case in federal court in Chattanooga.

The case was sent back to Dayton but the economic boom was over, and the adverse publicity image created by the trial resulted in the prosecution dismissing the case.

After the trial, Neal was a personal candidate for public office, running for United States Senator eighteen times, for governor in Tennessee nine times, and once for the House of Representatives. His last unsuccessful race was in 1954 when he ran for governor against Frank G. Clement. A fuller review of his life reveals that he was always a strong advocate for liberal cases. Perhaps his biggest contribution was his consistent advocacy for government control of the Tennessee River which ultimately led to the creation of the Tennessee Valley Authority.

He died on November 23, 1959, at the age of eighty-three and is buried in the Ault Cemetery in Roane County, Tennessee.

John Randolf Neal, Jr. and John T. Scopes

Monteagle's Most Notorious Visitor
Al Capone

The little community at the high point of the Cumberland Plateau, about 45 miles from Chattanooga and 90 miles from Nashville on Interstate I-24, has an intriguing history. Its citizens reside in the three Middle Tennessee counties of Grundy, Marion and Franklin.

The founder of the town was John Moffat who first came to the area around 1870 and was so impressed with its beauty that he purchased over 1,000 acres. He was a Scottish-Canadian temperance believer who became an active leader in the town. As a result, the town was originally named "Moffat Station" in his honor. It would later be changed to "Mount Eagle" and then to "Monteagle." Eventually, the spelling would become the present municipality known as Monteagle and it would be incorporated under that name in 1962.

Prior to I-24 being built as part of the Interstate system, Monteagle was part of the Dixie Highway which runs from Chicago, Illinois, to Miami, Florida, as Highway 41.

Due to the elevation of Monteagle being close to 2,000 feet above sea level prior to the construction of the freeway, the downward trip from the top of the Cumberland Mountain to the valley below on 41 was considered one of the most dangerous descents in the country. Many of the tractor trailer rigs would burn out their brakes and often run off the side of the mountain, resulting in injury, death and loss of cargo. Any truck driver who survived the "Deadman's Ride" down the mountain and lived to tell about it became part of the lore and mystique of the area.

With the completion of I-24 and the creation of some runaway truck ramps, the safety record of the area has drastically improved.

A part of the rumored history of Monteagle has been the "Mabee House." Whether fact or fiction, it makes an entertaining tale that places one of the most notorious criminals in the history of America as having a tie to Monteagle and the Mabee House.

Made of mountain stone and now a popular and fashionable restaurant named High Point, it still possesses the mysterious aura of its earlier history.

Felicia Irene Mabee was born in Monteagle in 1885 and was a descendant of a poor family who was able to build one of the largest homes in the community. Mystery and intrigue surrounds it. The big rock house is alleged to have been constructed on the site of a previous residence that had mountain stone added as an outside layer sometime between 1920 and 1930.

Little has ever been told about how Irene came into ownership of the house or how she was financially able to drive a big black Cadillac during the years before, during, and after the Depression.

Monteagle was close to the halfway point between Chicago and Miami, and it would be a good stop for travelers between those two destinations. There would be times when several large cars would arrive and take a respite from the long journey.

Rumors exist that a notorious gangster from Chicago bought the house for Irene, although there was an age difference of fifteen years between the older woman and the young criminal. Tales of alleged criminal activity at the house persisted in spite of lack of verification. Mountain folks during this time preferred to mind their own business and go their own way.

However, a couple of rumors supposedly have some actual contact with the Chicago mobster who was the most successful criminal in the underworld during the Prohibition Era between 1920-1933.

A local barber claimed that he had one time been called upon to cut the Chicagoan's hair.

The most direct rumor came from a local citizen who, one winter day, came upon a big car that had slid off the icy roads that exist on the mountain and was stuck in a ditch. The car was pulled out by the Good Samaritan using his team of oxen. When the driver of the car offered to pay for the tow, the owner of the team declined payment saying the mountain people didn't take money for helping folks in trouble.

Whereas the big man offered him a cigar and said, "My name is Al Capone. Call on me at any time."

Other rumors involve the presence of Al Capone on several occasions at the stone house in the 1920-1931 years prior to serving his income tax invasion sentence in Atlanta and Alcatraz and his death in 1947 in Miami at his home on Palm Island.

A recently discovered National Registry of Historic Places Registration Form filed on November 21, 1997, asking that the Irene Mabee (Gibson) House be placed on the national registry adds some additional corroboration of the Al Capone connection to the structure now known as High Point Restaurant.

Several interviews of Monteagle residents during the period of 1925-1931 indicate that Capone visited the 1875 Mabee home on a regular basis when he was traveling between Chicago and Miami. Allegedly there are existing photos showing "Big Al" in his car being pulled up Highway 41 from Pelham, Tennessee, in the late 1920's when the vehicle broke down. The photos give further corroboration of Capone's presence in the area.

Legends of secret tunnels, moonshine stills and acts of criminal activity still are attached to the stone house in Monteagle. Whether fact or fiction, they make a good story that adds to the atmosphere at High Point while visitors enjoy a good dinner.

Grundy County native and 1960 graduate of the University of the South at Sewanee, Ernie Cheek, refutes the Capone rumors in their entirety. Ernie claims a knowledgeable relationship with the Mabees but disavows any belief in the presence of Chicago's most notorious criminal on the Cumberland Plateau at Monteagle. The absence of any knowledge of the Capone stories is also supported by another lifelong resident of the area, Jack Baggenstoss.

Author Laurence Bergreen in his novel entitled *Capone: The Man and the Era,* (Simon and Schuster, pp. 701) presented the private side of the gangster as being very generous and well-liked outside of his "direct business and federal law enforcement."

It is a known fact that Irene Mabee (Gibson) and her mother, Marie, were residents of Chicago during the 1920's and could have met the notorious criminal during that era.

It has also been rumored that another famous gangster, John Dillinger in 1925, had stayed at the Beersheba Springs Hotel in Grundy County prior to his returning to Chicago and being gunned down by Elliott Ness and his G-Men as he came out of a movie theater.

Both of the fact or fiction scenarios add much to the mysterious history of the Cumberland Plateau.

Herschel P. Franks
Longest Serving State Judge

Hardin County, Tennessee, is the birthplace of the longest serving state judge prior to his retirement on December 31, 2012, as the presiding judge of the Tennessee Court of Appeals, Herschel Pickens Franks.

Born in Savannah, Tennessee, Judge Franks received an undergraduate degree from the University of Tennessee-Martin and the University of Maryland. After serving in the Air Force from 1950-1954, he received his law degree from the University of Tennessee at Knoxville in 1957. He migrated to Chattanooga in 1957 and practiced insurance defense law with the firm of Harris, Moon, Meacham and Franks. Well-liked by his fellow attorneys, he served as president of the Chattanooga Bar Association.

In 1970 he was appointed Chancellor in Hamilton County by Governor Buford Ellington and served in that capacity until 1978 when he was appointed to the Tennessee Court of Appeals by Governor Ray Blanton where he sat until 2012. The Court of Appeals is the intermediate appellate court, which handles all civil appeals before they can be appealed to the Tennessee Supreme Court.

Many lawyers feel that Judge Franks should have been on the Tennessee Supreme Court, but some infighting in the Tennessee Democratic Party, as well as some courageous but controversial decisions in high profile cases, created opposition that may have hurt his chances to be on the high court. Judge Franks always had the intestinal fortitude to make the tough decision if he thought he was right.

The landmark case of Paty v. McDaniel in the United States Supreme Court is only one of the areas of the law where Judge Franks' rulings overturned existing standards. He declared the Tennessee Constitutions provision barring ministers from serving as legislators in the Tennessee General Assembly violated their right to due process of law under the United States Constitution.

McDaniel, a popular African-American preacher, filed a petition to run as a delegate to the 1977 Tennessee Constitutional Convention. Attorney Selma Cash Paty filed suit to keep McDaniel off the ballot, and Judge Franks, in a very unpopular ruling, declared that the constitutional ban on ministers serving in elected positions was invalid. Said case was appealed to the United States Supreme Court which reversed the Tennessee Supreme Court in a 9-0 opinion. Said holding had other significant consequences as it launched Revered McDaniel's political career which included election to the governing board of Hamilton County government and also helped lead to a nine-member district-based County Commission to provide equal representation for all races. The number of ministers running for and being elected to public office has increased substantially since this decision in 1978.

Judge Franks also authored a controversial decision in the area of comatose patients on life support machines. It dealt with the responsibilities of family members to authorize medical care providers to unplug the patient from life support machines. In the face of opposition from the Tennessee Medical Society, he laid down a ruling which became instrumental in creating a national movement for living wills and right-to-die laws. Said standards are commonly used in today's society but were a novelty at the time of Judge Franks' ruling in the Tennessee courts.

He was not hesitant in ruling against a municipal judge who jailed an indigent defendant for contempt when she could not pay the fine or court costs she owed to the City of Chattanooga on the grounds that the defendant was illegally held and detained.

While Chancellor, he also handled a case involving James Earl Ray, the assassin of Dr. Marin Luther King, when Ray filed a *pro se* petition against two of his *habeas corpus* lawyers who he claimed refused to turn over his file after they were fired. The case was eventually settled between the parties by the return of the file. Ironically, when Ray's court-appointed lawyer turned the file over to the defendant at the state penitentiary in Nashville, Ray remarked, "This is the only time I have won anything in a court of law."

Franks also wrote the opinion in the case involving late Democratic gubernatorial candidate, John Jay Hooker, whose bright political star had dimmed over the years. Hooker was part of the special prosecution team headed by Jack Norman of Nashville that prosecuted Judge Raulston Schoolfield of Hamilton County in his impeachment proceedings in 1958. Hooker became somewhat of a political gadfly in his later years and filed suit against Governor Haslam in 2012 attacking the constitutionality of the Tennessee Retention Election Statute which governs how intermediate appellate (Tennessee Court of Appeals and Tennessee Court of Criminal Appeals) judges are elected.

In spite of the fact that two retired judges were appointed to hear the case, Judge Franks did not ask for a substitute judge and wrote the opinion that decided the case. His trial and appellate court decisions are full of courageous rulings where it is obvious that Judge Franks did not test the political winds prior to making a decision in cases that might have furthered or hindered his judicial career.

A lifelong Democrat, Judge Franks probably incurred more opposition within his own party than from Republicans. An untimely divorce, plus some professional jealousy, both contributed to his non-selection to be on the Tennessee Supreme Court. It was stated, "It's become axiomatic that had he been a Republican, he would have been appointed to the State Supreme Court years ago," according to one writer.

However, his adherence to his personal political philosophy and willingness to decide cases based solely on the law and facts demonstrates a type of judicial courage that ranks him high in the historical standings of judges who have served the State of Tennessee in a judicial capacity.

In 2019, biographical publisher Marquis presented Judge Franks with the Albert Nelson Marquis Lifetime Achievement Award. In 2009 Judge Franks received the Tennessee Bar Association highest service award to the judiciary – the Francis F. Drowota III Award.

He died March 19, 2020, at age of 89 and is buried in Chattanooga National Cemetery.

Frank W. Wilson
Federal District Judge Number One

Any attorney who practiced in the United State District Court for the Eastern District of Tennessee between the years of 1961-1982 can testify to the legal ability and high ethical standards of Judge Frank Wiley Wilson, who was appointed by President John F. Kennedy to fill the vacancy created by the elevation to senior status of Judge Leslie Darr on March 25, 1961.

Wilson was nominated for the office on May 24, 1961, and was confirmed by the United States Senate on June 15, 1961. The speed with which he was appointed was both a tribute to his legal ability and high moral ethics during a period of time when federal judgeships were filled without the political scrutiny and controversy by Congress today.

Judge Wilson was a native of Knoxville and a graduate of the University of Tennessee in 1939 and the College of Law in 1941. After serving in the military in the United States Army Air Force as a Sergeant from 1941-1946, he returned to Oak Ridge to re-enter the practice of law with attorney Eugene Joyce.

Active in the Democratic Party as a Southern Conservative, he ran unsuccessfully for Congress from the Second Congressional District against Howard Baker, Sr., in 1950. He remained an active Democrat in the heavily Republican District and supported Democratic Senatorial candidate Estes Kefauver when Kefauver defeated incumbent Senator Tom Stewart in the 1948 Democratic primary "coonskin cap" campaign. Kefauver put on a fur hat and, in a televised speech, refuted political boss E.H. Crump of Memphis' accusation that Kefauver was working for the "pinkos."

With the help of his law partner, Eugene Joyce, they also worked on behalf of Senator Albert Gore, Sr. and Senator John F. Kennedy of Massachusetts in 1960. As a result, he was selected to be federal judge for the federal vacancy in Chattanooga when Judge Darr retired. A condition of the appointment was that the new judge would have to live in Chattanooga.

The positive accolades attributed to Judge Wilson are too many to list in this short article. A long-overdue treatise on his life is being prepared by retired Hamilton County Circuit Judge, Neil Thomas, Jr., and is expected to cover the entire life of Judge Wilson.

During his career he handled many high profile cases, including the Jimmy Hoffa criminal trial, school desegregation, the teaching of the Bible in Hamilton County and City of Chattanooga public schools, and the First Amendment case of the Broadway play, "Hair," that played at the Memorial Auditorium.

While the general public and criminal defendants usually saw the professional side of Judge Wilson, there was much more about his personality. His involvement in many charitable and public institutions was extensive but not well known. While known as a tough sentencer in criminal cases, he kept touch with the individuals that he sentenced to the federal penitentiary. He corresponded with them regularly and encouraged them to do better. His visits to federal prisons to see prisoners was known to only a few close allies and his family.

A teetotaler and dedicated Methodist, he and his wife, Helen, would frown upon the efforts of one of his strongest political supporters who attempted to bring liquor into the Wilson home when he stayed with them.

He controlled his court room with dignity, was widely respected, and appreciated lawyers who were prepared and tried a good case before him.

Possessor of a coy sense of humor, he could always absorb a joke about himself when he made one of his infrequent courtroom blunders. In the "Hair" obscenity case, after the defense introduced a number of pornographic magazines and sex toys to show what was readily available in the Hamilton County area, Judge Wilson instructed the jury that they would be adjourned for the day and, "The Court would look after the evidence overnight." When the jury and courtroom spectators and attorneys burst into laughter, he sheepishly corrected his statement to mean that the exhibits would be locked up by the clerk of the court.

The most famous of his many trials during the twenty-one years he was on the federal bench had to be the Jimmy Hoffa criminal trial. The labor leader's defense team continuously attempted to provoke Judge

Wilson and to cause a mistrial. In spite of those tactics, he maintained his calm demeanor and gave all parties a fair trial. As a result of the tension and stress created by the tactics of the defense during the six-week trial, he suffered a severe heart attack.

Always a workaholic, he returned to the bench and would conduct civil pre-trial conferences lying on a couch in his office during a recess of a case on trial or during jury deliberations in another case. It was remarked by family and friends that the tension of the Hoffa trial took ten years off his life. He died on September 29, 1982.

Two significant events took place in his life that vividly demonstrate the honor and respect that he held in the judicial and legal communities.

The July 1980 issue of the national magazine "The American Lawyer" contained an article titled "The Best and Worse Federal Judges." Frank Wilson was selected as the Sixth Circuit's best judge in the four states of Michigan, Ohio, Kentucky and Tennessee.

A rare tribute to a lifelong Democrat like Frank Wilson was paid to Judge Wilson when he was selected to be one of five nominees to fill a vacancy on the United States Supreme Court in 1975 and invited to the White House by Republican President Gerald Ford for an interview.

Judge Frank Wilson set the standard for excellence as a federal judge which all judicial officers since have tried to imitate. The book that Judge Neil Thomas is preparing will provide substantial additional information on the interesting life of Judge Wilson as a lawyer, judge, politician, community leader, husband and father.

Judge Frank Wiley Wilson as pictured in the *New York Times* during the Hoffa trial.

David McKendree Key
Chattanooga's 1st Federal District Judge

David McKendree Key (January 27, 1824-February 3, 1900) was a Democratic United States Senator from Tennessee from 1875 to 1877. He was also a state Chancellor (judge) as well as the United States Postmaster General under President Rutherford B. Hayes.

From 1880 until 1895 he served as the United States District Judge for both the Eastern and Middle Districts of Tennessee as the first federal judge from Chattanooga.

Key was born in Greene County in upper East Tennessee, but the family moved to Monroe County in 1826 where he was reared. He graduated from Hiwassee College in 1859 and read with another attorney to be admitted to the practice of law.

He and his family moved to Chattanooga in 1853. Key entered the Civil War on the Confederacy side and eventually rose through the ranks to become a Lieutenant Colonel prior to the end of hostilities. Returning to Chattanooga he reentered the practice of law. In 1870 he served in the Tennessee state constitutional convention and that same year was elected as a Democratic Chancellor.

He ran unsuccessfully for the House of Representatives in 1872 while a sitting judge but resigned his judgeship in 1875 to accept an appointment to the United States Senate by Tennessee Governor James D. Porter. The vacancy was created by the death of former President Andrew Johnson.

Key was closely aligned with President Rutherford B. Hayes, and after he was defeated in the next election in the Tennessee General Assembly to retain his Washington Senate seat, he was appointed Postmaster General by the president and served from 1877 to 1880.

It was during this period of service that Key received strong criticism for his performances as postmaster general by Mark Twain (Samuel Clemens) in *The Autobiography of Mark Twain* published in 2010 after Twain had directed it not be released to the public until he had been dead for 100 years (1910-date of his death).

In spite of Twain's criticism, Hayes nominated Key to a federal judgeship in both the Middle and Eastern District of Tennessee at Chattanooga upon the death of Connally F. Trigg in 1880. After he was confirmed by the Senate, Key served in that capacity until 1895 and died in 1900. He is buried in Forrest Hills Cemetery.

On August 8, 1885, Chattanooga conducted a memorial service for Ulysses S. Grant who had successfully led the Union Army to victory at the Battle of Missionary Ridge in November, 1863. The main address was given by Judge Key, and he regaled the audience by alternatively paying tribute to the character of Grant as both general and president and by also telling numerous anecdotes about Grant.

As a final compliment to his former war opponent, Key stated, "My friends, the brightest star has fallen from our nation's firmament, but the story of its luster and beauty shall live as long as history shall last."

During his tenure as judge, Key was noted for seeking justice rather than for adhering to the strict letter of the law.

Of his twenty-four years of public service Judge Key spent twenty years on the bench either as a state or federal judge.

Judge Key handled many cases involving violations of the liquor laws in the illicit manufacturing of liquor (moonshine) which was produced in substantial quantity by the mountaineers of East Tennessee.

Applying his practical sense Judge Key, after a defendant was convicted, he would often allow him to return home to finish harvesting the crops in exchange for his promise that the offender would return to the next term of court for sentencing. Judge Key was fond of saying that not one offender had ever broken faith with him!

He had married Elizabeth L. Lenoir in 1857, and they had eight (8) children. She was the daughter of General Albert S. Lenoir of Loudon County, Tennessee, for whom Lenoir City is named.

In 1967 David Abshire wrote a book entitled *The South Rejects a Prophet: The Life of Senator D.M. Key* which was published by the F.A. Prager Company in New York. It describes in greater detail the interesting life of the first federal district judge from Chattanooga.

Tennessee's United States Supreme Court Justices

In the history of the Volunteer State only six men have occupied a seat on the United States Supreme Court. Unlike the spirited and confrontational hearings of today that occur in each Senate hearing on the evaluation of a potential supreme court justice, judicial appointments in the past were relatively simple. The president's nominees were normally affirmed with the advise and consent of the Senate rather quickly.

Howell Edmunds Jackson (1832-1895)

The first Tennessean to be selected to serve on the United States Supreme Court was Howell Edmunds Jackson who was born in Paris, Tennessee, and later practiced law in Jackson. He was a graduate of Cumberland School of Law in Lebanon, Tennessee, in 1856.

Jackson served in the Civil War for the South as a civil receiver of property confiscated from Unionists. After the war was over he moved to Memphis, took on a new law partner, and they created a successful civil practice including the representation of railroads, banks and northern business interests.

After his first wife, Sophia, died of yellow fever in 1873, he married Mary Harding of Nashville. Her father gave them 2,200 acres of land, but was unable to make the enterprise successful.

Moving back to Memphis, he was elected to the Tennessee House of Representatives in 1890 and would also serve in the United States Senate from 1881-1886.

In 1886 he accepted an appointment by President Grover Cleveland to the United States Circuit Court for the Sixth Circuit where he served until 1893 when President Benjamin Harrison nominated Jackson to be an Associate Justice of the Supreme Court of the United States.

During his tenure on the Highest Court, Jackson wrote forty-six opinions and four dissents. Because of his business law experience representing his previous clients in Memphis, he had experience in patent cases. His knowledge was helpful to the Court since there was several cases of that type on his docket.

After only one year on the Court, Jackson contacted tuberculosis and was contemplating retirement but improved successfully to cast his final vote on the constitutionality of the national income tax passed in 1894, which imposed 2% taxes on income over $4,000.00. The Court struck down the tax as being unconstitutional, but Jackson voted with the minority and wrote a blistering dissent claiming that it, "Was the most disastrous blow ever struck at the Constitutional power of Congress!" Only three months passed before Jackson died in Nashville and was buried in the Mount Olivet Cemetery.

John Catron (1786-1865)

The second Tennessean to serve on the United States Supreme Court was John Catron who was nominated by President Andrew Jackson in 1837 and served until 1865. Catron's early life was kind of a mystery, and little is known about it except that his family had emigrated from Germany to Virginia.

He had served under Jackson during the War of 1812. After reading law under a licensed attorney, he was admitted to the Tennessee bar in 1815. As a slave holder Catron impregnated a slave, Sally, who was owned by another family in Nashville. She bore Catron a son, James, who would later become an educated and successful landholder.

James also practiced law in Sparta from 1815-1818, serving as both a part-time prosecutor and also engaging in the civil practice of law. He later moved to Nashville and had a law practice there until 1824.

From 1824-1834 Catron served on the Tennessee Supreme Court of Errors and Appeals (Tennessee Supreme Court) and became Chief Justice in 1831. In 1834 the Tennessee State Legislature abolished the position of chief justice, and Catron retired from the court. Whether it was in any way related to Catron directing Martin Van Buren's presidential campaign against fellow Tennessean Hugh Lawson White may have been a political factor.

After returning to the practice of law, President Andrew Jackson on his last day in office on March 3, 1837, nominated Catron to be a justice on the United States Supreme Court where he served for twenty-eight years before dying in 1865.

Catron wrote few opinions but did side with the majority in the Dred Scott v. Sanford case approving slavery. However, he opposed succession from the Union by Tennessee. His political views in his decision primarily coincided with those of President Jackson.

His views on corporation control changed over the years. While he initially supported the rights of corporations, he developed overpowering anti-corporate views in his later years on the court. Catron argued that the power of corporations should be subservient to that of the federal government.

Although a slave owner, he strongly supported Jackson's view that the Union should be preserved at all costs. This position placed his life in danger, and he had to flee Nashville and reside in Kentucky. Catron maintained his support of the rights of states and preserving the Federal Union throughout his life. He was consistent in his criticism of the national bank, a supporter of federal power, and a pro-Union, pro-slavery supporter.

This complex justice died in 1865 at the age of seventy-nine and is buried in the Mount Olivet Cemetery in Nashville.

Horace Harmon Lurton (1844-1914)

The third Tennessean to be appointed as an Associate Justice of the United States Supreme Court was Horace Harmon Lurton who was twice captured by Union forces and the second time was a prisoner of war at Johnson's Island Prison Camp in Sandusky Bay, Ohio. He was later paroled by President Abraham Lincoln, and there is a conflict in the reasons for his parole. Lurton claimed that the desperate pleas for mercy from his mother convinced the president to release him from prison.

An article in the December 1994 edition of the *Civil War Times,* by historian Roger Long, stated that Lurton received his parole from Johnson's Island only when he signed an oath of allegiance to the Union and not because of any action by President Lincoln.

Justice Lurton was born on February 26, 1844, in Newport, Kentucky, and received a law degree in 1867 from Cumberland University in Lebanon, Tennessee. He entered the private practice of law in Clarksville, Tennessee until 1875 when he became Chancellor for the Sixth Judicial District and served until 1878.

After re-entry into the practice of law from 1878 to 1886, he became a member of the Tennessee Supreme Court and served until 1893. President Grover Cleveland on March 22, 1893, appointed Lurton to a seat on the Sixth Circuit of Appeals. He would serve on that court until December 13, 1909, when he was nominated by President William Howard Taft as one of his five appointees on the United States Supreme Court. The nomination surprised some court followers because Lurton was a Democrat whereas Taft was a Republican.

Taft would later explain his selection of Lurton, "The chief pleasure of my administration," was the appointment of Lurton.

Lurton's closest colleague on the High Court in judicial philosophy was Associate Justice Oliver Wendell Holmes as a progressive. The most notable opinion that Lurton wrote during his short tenure of four years on the court was Coyle v. Smith, 221 U.S. 559 (1911) which held that the federal government could not dictate to a state where their capitol should be located, as all states must be on "equal footing."

On July 12, 1914, Lurton suffered a heart attack and died while in Atlantic City, New Jersey, and is buried in Greenwood Cemetery in Clarksville, Tennessee.

Edward Terry Sanford (1865-1930)

Edward Terry Sanford was a native east Tennessean having been born in Knoxville on July 23, 1865, at the close of the Civil War. He was the son of a prominent family whose father was president or vice president of nearly twelve banks and corporations. He was both a graduate of the University of Tennessee and of Harvard Law School in 1889. Sanford developed a successful law practice in Knoxville with the help of his father's influence and engaged in private practice in that city from 1890 to 1907.

His first public service was as special assistant to the Attorney General of the United States from 1905 to 1907 and then as Assistant Attorney General in 1907. It was during that year that he became chief prosecutor in the case of the United States v. Shipp, arising out of the contempt charges place against the Sheriff of Hamilton County, Tennessee for not protecting a young black male from being lynched on the Walnut Street Bridge in downtown Chattanooga. Sheriff Joseph Shipp and several others were successfully prosecuted by Sanford. It is the only criminal case ever tried by the United States Supreme Court.

In 1908 Sanford was nominated by President Theodore Roosevelt to a joint seat on the United States District Court for the Eastern District of Tennessee and the United States District Court for the Western District of Tennessee. He would serve in that capacity until President Warren Harding nominated him to the United States Supreme Court in 1923. He would be an associate justice for seven years until his death in 1930.

Justice Sanford wrote 130 opinions during his seven-year tenure on the court. His landmark opinion in the case of Gitlow vs. New York implied that some provisions of the free speech provisions of the Bill of Rights would apply equally with equal force to the states via the Due Process Clause of the Fourteenth Amendment. This opinion would lead to the "nationalization" of the Bill of Rights during the Earl Warren Court in analyzing other sections of said document.

Chief Justice William Howard Taft was often referred to as Sanford's mentor, and they often sided together in opinions. Both would be part of the court's "conservative" body. Sanford died suddenly on March 8, 1930, of uremic poisoning shortly after a tooth extraction. Ironically his death occurred just a few hours before the death of his beloved colleague, Chief Justice Taft. Sanford is buried at Greenwood Cemetery in Knoxville. For more information, a biography, *Edward TerrySanford: A Tenessean of the U.S. Supreme Court*, by Stepahanie L. Slater, is availabel from University of Tennesse Press or on Amazon.com.

James Clark McReynolds (1862-1946)

The fourth member of the United States Supreme Court from Tennessee, James Clark McReynolds, served on the Court from 1914 to his retirement in 1941. He also served as United States Attorney General under President Woodrow Wilson. Although he was born in Elkton, Kentucky, after graduating from the University of Virginia Law School he moved to Nashville, Tennessee, where he served as an Adjunct Professor of Law at Vanderbilt Law School for three years.

Active in politics, he was an unsuccessful candidate for Congress in 1896 and that same year headed the Tennessee delegation to the Democratic convention. Under President Theodore Roosevelt, he served as Assistant Attorney General from 1903-1907. McReynolds was an expert in anti-trust matters and was often retained by the government to file cases in that field of law. He was particularly successful in matters against the "Tobacco Trust."

On March 15, 1913, he was appointed as the forty-eighth United States Attorney General where he served until appointed to the United States Supreme Court on August 19, 1914. During his 27 years on the High Court, he authored 506 opinions plus 157 dissents. He was a thorn in the side of Franklin Delano Roosevelt's New Deal, as he wrote 93 dissents against the legislation proposed by Franklin D. Roosevelt.

McReynolds was continuously in conflict with the other justices and was labeled "Scrooge" by national journalist Drew Pearson. He was called a bigot, prejudiced, and earned the reputation of being someone who seemed to take pleasure in making others uncomfortable. His prejudices extended to his selection of law clerks, as he would only select white males to work for him.

One of his displays of prejudice against Jews was his dislike of Associate Justice Louis Brandeis, the first Jewish member of the court. McReynolds would not speak to him for three years after Brandeis' appointment. McReynolds' list of prejudices had no limits. Race, smoking, segregation, sexism were all part of his makeup which created discord on the Court.

McReynolds died alone on August 24, 1946, in a hospital without a single friend or relative present. In death a tribute by the *Christian Science Monitor* praised McReynolds as being, "The last and lone champion on the Supreme Bench battling the steady encroachment of Federal powers on State and individual rights."

Abraham Fortas (1910-1982)

It is unfortunate that Tennessee's sixth and last appointment to the United States Supreme Court had both a brilliant legal career as well as ethics problems that led to his resignation in 1969 after only four years of service. Fortas giving up his seat on the High Court would allow President Nixon to appoint Republican conservative Warren Burger Chief Justice, and this ended the liberal philosophy that had begun when President Eisenhower had appointed Earl Warren of California as Chief Justice.

Fortas was a close confidant and attorney for President Lyndon Johnson beginning with Johnson's contested election race for a Senate seat from Texas. When Johnson became president, he had appointed Associate Justice Arthur Goldberg ambassador to the United Nations in order that he could recommend Fortas to be appointed in his place. Abe Fortas was born on June 19, 1910, in Memphis and attended South Side High School, Southwestern at Memphis (Rhodes), and Yale Law School, earning top academic honors at all three.

During the Franklin Roosevelt Administration, he served as general counsel of the Public Works Administration and as Undersecretary of the Interior. Under President Truman, he was appointed to be an advisor to the delegation organizing the United Nations. In 1946 he founded Arnold & Fortas and was successful in arguing the landmark case in 1963 of Guedon v. Wainwright in the United States Supreme court which held that state courts are required under the Sixth Amendment to provide lawyers in criminal cases for defendants unable to afford their own attorneys.

Fortas' close relationship with President Johnson was one of the main reasons that he was criticized during his confirmation hearings in the United States Senate. The fact that he had accepted $15,000 for nine speaking engagements at American University's Washing College of Law plus his acceptance of $20,000 in 1966 from the family foundation of Wall Street financier Lewis Wolfson, a friend and former client who was under investigation for securities violations, intensified the opposition from his confirmation foes.

Fortas barely received a majority vote to end the filibuster against his appointment to be Chief Justice. Fortas that same day asked President Johnson to withdraw his nomination. Fortas' later resignation in 1969 allowed President Nixon to appoint another conservative, Harry Blackmon, to the Bench and to reshape the political makeup. Fortas would return to the private practice of law and would argue several cases before the Court that he had left. The rise and fall of Abe Fortas would be acknowledged as one of the biggest turnabouts in the history of the United States Supreme Court.

Ellis K. Meacham
Author & Judge

Although his Pulitzer Prize winning grandson, Jon Meacham, is better known in the literary world for his biography *American Lion: Andrew Jackson in the White House in 2009,* the late Chattanooga Ellis K. Meacham also made significant contributions with his writings.

Ellis was born in Chattanooga in 1913 and died in 1998. He was the son of an attorney, graduated from the University of Chattanooga (U.C.) in 1935 and received a law degree from Vanderbilt University in 1937. He entered the practice of law with the firm of Cantrell, Meacham and Moon as a young associate attorney.

In 1940, he married Jean Austin, a teacher and future dean at U.C. She would be a supporter of his writing endeavors and would later create the Meacham Writers Workshop in 1985 in honor of Ellis at the University of Chattanooga and Chattanooga State Community College. The workshop is held twice a year and gives novice writers an opportunity to interact with experienced writers of national renown.

During World War II, Ellis served in the Navy as a gunnery officer in the Pacific and obtained the rank of Commander. He returned to the practice of law in Chattanooga as an assistant city attorney in 1948. He practiced with his father C.W.K. Meacham until the latter retired in 1954.

In January 1958, Ellis became a member of a newly created law firm, Anderson, Meacham and Collins. Meacham was an assistant city attorney under City Attorney Joe Anderson who had served as a member of the city's legal staff since 1920.

Eugene Collins, who had served two terms in the Tennessee General Assembly representing Hamilton County, would replace Joe Anderson when he retired as City Attorney. Collins would retain that position from 1963-1990. He died in April 26, 2004.

Aside from his law practice, Meacham continued to write and in 1968 published the first novel in his Napoleonic nautical trilogy set in India and in the style of the more famous Horatio Hornblower series. His lead character was Percival Mereweather. *The East Indiaman* (1968) was followed by *On the Company's Service* (1971) and *For King and Country* (1976). His first book won him a Friends of American Writers Major Award in fiction in 1969.

In 1968, he was employed as an assistant city attorney for the City of Chattanooga. In 1972, he became judge in the City Court of Chattanooga handling traffic, criminal, misdemeanor, and felony bind-over cases until he retired.

During this time, he was also working on a proposed book on the 1906 case involving the hanging of African-American Ed Johnson from the Walnut Street Bridge in Chattanooga arising out of a later determined false charge of rape of a white woman. This led to the historical trial against the sheriff of Hamilton County and others for contempt of court for allowing Johnson to be taken out of the Hamilton County Jail and hanged.

Meacham was a close friend of attorneys Crawford Bean and his younger partner, Leroy Phillips, Jr., and decided to curtail his writing activities. According to legal sources, he turned over his preliminary investigation file on the case to Leroy. This led to completion of the story and the collaboration of Leroy Phillips and nationally recognized legal writer, Mark Curriden, who together wrote the award-winning book, *Contempt of Court.* That book later resulted in the posthumous vindication of Ed Johnson by the Criminal Court of Hamilton County on the charge of rape in 2006. Phillips and Curriden would be recognized by winning an American Bar Association Silver Gavel Award for the book.

After Meacham became City Judge, he realized that he had less time to write and never finished the proposed fourth volume of the Mereweather nautical series. He also started a fictionalized account of the Jimmy Hoffa trial held in Chattanooga in 1968 but stopped work on it prior to completion.

In 1998 Ellis Meacham died, having made significant contributions in the field of literature and law. The Meacham Writers Workshop insures possible greater recognition of his writings after his death than he achieved during his lifetime.

When Sergeant York Came to Chattanooga

On May 29, 2019, the nation's greatest World War I hero came to Chattanooga as an honored guest for a two day stay at the luxurious Patten Hotel.

The reception that 31 year-old Sergeant Alvin York received when his train pulled into the Terminal Station was much more than he could have ever expected. Hundreds of well-wishers carrying flowers clogged the train station as the hero from Pall Mall, Tennessee, in Fentress County arrived.

The Congressional Medal of Honor winner, who also had won numerous awards from the Allied Nations, fought against Germany was given accommodations in two of the nicest rooms at the hotel. A barber and manicurist prepared Sgt. York for his appearance at the weekly Rotary luncheon before a crowd of 300 attendees. After being eulogized by several speakers, Sgt. York was made an honorary Rotarian and appointed a delegate to the Rotary International convention in Salt Lake City. York humbly addressed the audience by simply saying, "I am just a soldier boy."

However his exploits were described by the Allied commander-in-chief, General Pershing, as the greatest thing accomplished by any private soldier of all the armies of Europe.

He had refused to sell for commercial gain his version of his feats. However Sgt. York did agree to give his audience an abbreviated version of the heroics that resulted in his becoming the most highly decorated soldier of World War I. Although he had originally sought exemption from serving in active battle on the grounds of being a conscientious objector, as a member of the 82nd Infantry Division, he had single-handedly crushed a German machine gun battalion. He killed at least 25 enemy soldiers and captured 132 prisoners.

In addition to the Medal of Honor he was awarded the *Croix de Guerre*, the highest French decoration for bravery in action.

Twenty years later, he agreed to cooperate in the filming of his life story in the 1941 Academy Award winning movie for which the Best

Actor award went to Gary Cooper. A stipulation of making of the movie was that royalties go to the York Foundation to support an industrial and Bible school near York's farm. Both continue today as part of York Institution as a public high school in Jamestown, Tennessee, after being transferred to the State of Tennessee in 1937.

Alvin C. York died on September 2, 1964, in a Nashville Hospital after a 10 year illness.

Sergeant Alvin C. York

Ray E. Duke
Whitwell's Medal of Honor Hero

The small community of Whitwell in Marion County, Tennessee, is appropriately proud that one of its citizens gave his life in the service of his country in the Korean conflict and was awarded the Congressional Medal of Honor. The Medal was posthumously awarded to his family on March 19, 1954.

Ray Eugene Duke was born in Whitwell on May 9, 1923, and died while a prisoner of war on November 11, 1951. His heroic action took place near Mugok, Korea, on April 26, 1951.

Duke had served in the United States Army in World War II and was a Sergeant First Class during the Korean conflict. Upon being informed that several men in his platoon had been isolated by the enemy and were in the process of being annihilated, Duke led a small force in a daring assault which re-captured the area from the enemy.

In a follow-up attack by a large force of North Koreans, Sgt. Duke was wounded by mortar fire. Despite his injuries he confidently encouraged his men to hold their positions in spite of being subjected to extreme firepower by the enemy.

Wounded a second time, Duke received battlefield first aid and returned to his position.

The ferocious attacks were renewed the next morning, and Duke remained in charge of his men. In spite of his wounds, Ray repeatedly braved enemy force to move amongst his men to instill confidence. During the action he was wounded a third time in both legs and was unable to walk. "Realizing that he was impeding the progress up the hill, he urged them to leave him and seek safety."

As his fellow soldiers retreated to their own safety, Ray was last seen pouring devastating gun fire into the on-pushing North Koreans.

He was subsequently taken prisoner and died as a prisoner of war several months later.

Duke was awarded the Medal of Honor, Purple Heart, Combat Infantryman's Badge, Prisoner of War Medal, Korean Service Medal, United Nations Service Medal, Nationals Defense Service Medal, Koreans Presidential Unit Citation, Republic of Korea War Service Medal, in addition to the World War II Victory Medal.

His remains were eventually returned to the United States and he was buried in the Chattanooga National Cemetery with full military honors.

Although he had received less public acclaim than many of the other Medal of Honor recipients from this area, his display of courage and protection of his men after being wounded three times is a living monument to his dedication to the military service in defense of our country.

Sergeant Ray Eugene Duke

Raymond H. Cooley
Dunlap's Medal Of Honor

One of many acts of extraordinary individual courage in World War II was performed by a native of Dunlap, Tennessee, Staff Sergeant Raymond H. Cooley. Born on May 14, 1916, Cooley entered the United States Army in Richard City, Tennessee, outside of South Pittsburg. He quickly rose through the ranks to become a Staff Sergeant. He earned the Medal of Honor in a battle which occurred at Luzon, Philippines, on February 24, 1945.

Raymond H. Cooley

Cooley was the leader of a platoon that was assigned the task of knocking out the Japanese observation point that had been harassing American positions. After an extensive search through the jungle, the well-protected outpost was located at the end of the day, and the platoon camped the night of the 23rd within approximately 300 yards of the heavily fortified position.

The next morning, Cooley's platoon attacked, but their advance was soon slowed down by heavy machine gun fire from two locations. The gun placements were also protected by riflemen firing from slit trenches on the hillside. All of the advancing American soldiers were pinned down by the withering gunfire except Cooley, who continued to advance throwing hand grenades.

Due to the heavy concentration of enemy fire, Cooley did not hold the grenades the maximum number of seconds after pulling the pins and hurling them at the enemy. As a result, the Japanese threw several back at Cooley. As his advance was being imperiled by the re-thrown grenades, Cooley wisely delayed the timing of his release of the deadly weapons.

By holding the grenade for three seconds before throwing the grenades towards the Japanese, he was able to stop the dangerous game of "playing catch" with his foes. Cooley destroyed one enemy gun nest and then advanced to wipe out a second.

Raymond was joined by several of his fellow soldiers, and the Japanese rushed towards him and his men screaming like savages. As he attempted to throw another grenade, he was surrounded by both his fellow soldiers and the Japanese. Having pulled the pin, he could not find a place to hurl the grenade without endangering the lives of his buddies. In a moment of valor that would eventually become a part of his historic display of devotion to his fellow soldiers, Sergeant Cooley "gripped his right hand over the grenade....and shoved the missile beneath the stock of his rifle."

After the grenade exploded, Cooley suffered the loss of his right hand and sustained other wounds in the forehead, right eye, nose, both shoulders, right thigh and his stomach.

He underwent a long rehabilitation period and received medical treatment from field and base hospitals and McCroskey Hospital in Temple, Texas.

Cooley was awarded the Purple Heart Award along with several other medals and ribbons and was decorated by President Harry S. Truman on August 23, 1945, along with 27 other military heroes in the courtroom of the White House in Washington, D.C. Truman stated that he, "Considered winning the Medal of Honor, a bigger award than being President."

Cooley wore the Purple Heart Medal, the combat infantryman's badge, the Asiatic-Pacific theatre ribbon with three major battles participation stars, the pre-Pearl Harbor ribbon, good conduct ribbon and the Philippines liberation ribbon.

Before the Philippines battles, Cooley participated in the battles of Guadalcanal and the New Guinea invasion. Sgt. Cooley proudly served with the 25th Division, 27th Infantry, Co. B of the Army.

Unfortunately, the seriousness of his war injuries resulted in Cooley becoming addicted to drugs and alcohol. He was killed in a one-car accident on March 12, 1947, when his convertible coupe ran into a tree and landed in a ditch. He was buried in the National Cemetery in Chattanooga with full military honors.

In 2017, the Tennessee legislature, upon request of the City Commission of Dunlap and State Representative Ron Travis, officially named state highway 28 between Jasper and I-24 as the Raymond H. Cooley Highway.

Charles "Duke" Pearman
Korean War POW

The Southeast Tennessee area has had many war heroes in both World Wars and Korea. The acts of courage of Charles Coolidge of Signal Mountain, Tennessee, Desmond Doss of Flintstone, Georgia, and Paul Huff of Cleveland, Tennessee, have been well documented in the news media over the years and the accolades are well deserved.

However, there is a young man from Athens, Tennessee, who along with thousands of other young soldiers participated in the Korean War conflict and was captured after eight months of service to his country. He was incarcerated as a prisoner of war for twenty-eight months. He was released on August 10, 1953, after a cease fire agreement was reached with the North and South Koreans and allied forces on both sides.

Although not recognized as a decorated war hero, Corporal Charles "Duke" Pearman was not forgotten by his hometown of Athens, Tennessee, and on October 1, 1953, a parade was held in his honor. Flanked by his father and uncle in an open Cadillac convertible, "He smiled only slightly as he nodded to the cheering hundreds of citizens assembled along the parade route in downtown Athens," according to the *Daily Post Athenian.*

In an article in the *Chattanooga Times* in August 1993 entitled "Athens Honored a POW in 1953," reporter Bill Casteel described the events of the celebration on October 1, 1953. Some two thousand citizens turned out to unroll the welcome mat for Athens' only known soldier who had been held captive by the North Koreans.

At the end of the parade route, a ceremony presided over by Mayor J.P. Cartwright took place at the McMinn County Courthouse. Duke was presented with several items including a $500.00 war bond, a key to the city, a scroll with the names of several hundred well-wishers, numerous gift certificates by local merchants, and membership cards in the local American Legion and Veteran of Foreign War by the local chapters.

Pearman later moved to Winter Haven, Florida, and became a successful carpenter. Like many POWs who survived the war, he received a large amount of back pay. He related that he bought a new Ford automobile and started drinking. A bad automobile accident that almost resulted in his death changed his involvement with alcohol. He subsequently joined a church, became an ordained preacher, and restored several area churches for approximately twenty-four years before going into construction work.

Years later Pearman recalled that he wished he could go back to Athens and thank the persons who set up and conducted the parade that honored him for his military service. He had realized, "It means so much more to me now than it did back then."

Duke Pearman's experience was a reminder that every young man who served his country was a hero, although not all were recognized and honored by their hometown. Fortunately, Athens, Tennessee, on October 1, 1953, was one that did.

Charles "Duke" Pearman

Raymond Austin Prater
Audie Murphy's Chattanooga Connection

Much has been written of the heroic exploits of Tennessee Medal of Honor winners, Alvin York (WWI), Charles Coolidge, Desmond Doss and Paul Huff (WWII).

Movies have been made about the military exploits of Sergeant York and recently about conscientious objector, Doss. Sometime in the future, the acts of bravery of Coolidge and Huff may be preserved in cinema.

Chattanooga has established a National Medal of Honor Heritage Center located at 2 Aquarium Way in downtown Chattanooga next to the Tennessee Aquarium.

Although not a Tennessean, another Medal of Honor winner had legitimate ties to Chattanooga through attorney Raymond Austin Prater.

Prater was a 1941 graduate of Tyner High School. He served in the Army from 1942-1946, graduated from Washington and Lee Law School in Virginia, and opened a law practice in Chattanooga in 1950 with offices in the Chattanooga Bank Building. He unsuccessfully ran for Congress in 1952 and 1962 as a Democrat and was co-manager of the Hamilton County campaign of President John F. Kennedy in 1960. During his military career, he fought in the Battle of the Bulge and was awarded a Purple Heart and Combat Infantry Badge.

Raymond Prater

Prater was politically ambitious and aligned himself with the enemies of controversial Criminal Court Judge Raulston Schoolfield who was successfully impeached in 1958 on three minor charges and was disbarred from the practice of law in 1961. Prater had initially approached Judge Schoolfield about running for Congress in the 1952 race in the Democratic Primary. He asked the judge for his political support.

Schoolfield is alleged to have told Prater that he should not run for two reasons: 1.) He was too young; and 2.) He needed some legislative experience and suggested that he run for the Tennessee General Assembly for his first political attempt. Prater was not receptive to that advice and became an outspoken enemy of Schoolfield.

In 1962 Prater ran again, and he finished a distant third behind J.B. Frazier and Wilkes T. Thrasher, Jr. Thrasher had upset Frazier and then lost to political newcomer, Republican William (Bill) Brock, III. Prater in 1962 only received 2,658 votes but may have provided the margin of defeat for Frazier who only lost to Thrasher by 269 votes (36,055 to 35,786).

Prater continued his involvement in Democratic politics, and it has been alleged that he was requested by Attorney General Robert Kennedy to screen the jury pool for the government in the Jimmy Hoffa trial in Chattanooga in 1968. A previous trial in Nashville had resulted in a mistrial because of jury tampering.

Prater was killed in a small place crash near Roanoke, Virginia, on May 28, 1971, along with the pilot and four other passengers including World War II Medal of Honor recipient and movie star, Audie Murphy. The pilot had his private pilot license, 8,000 hours of flying time, but no instrument rating. The plane crashed into Brush Mountain in bad weather.

The life story of Audie Murphy has been well documented in literature and songs. He was an underage teenager who lied about his age to get into the Army in World War II. In numerous battles in Italy and Europe against the Germans, he was awarded a total of thirty-three medals by the American, French, and Belgium governments to become the most highly decorated soldier of that war.

Audie Murphey

The ill-fated flight had left Atlanta, Georgia, in the morning, and the plane was on its way to a Modular Management Plant at Martinsville, Virginia.

Raymond Prater was identified in an article in the *Chattanooga Times* on May 31, 1971, as "general legal counsel for Modular Management, Inc."

Family members of Prater also claimed that he was a "lawyer and adviser to WWII hero and movie star, Audie Murphy." The extent of that relationship is somewhat contradicted in an article in the *Chattanooga Times* on May 31, 1971, where Murphy was identified as "representing himself and two groups of prospective investors."

Irrespective of their relationship, both of the decorated World War II soldiers died in the same plane crash. Murphy was 46 and Prater was 48.

Prior to his death, Murphy acted in forty movies. The majority of his roles were in westerns. He played himself in the 1955 autobiographical portrayal of his life, "To Hell and Back." Although not a polished actor, Murphy did receive favorable reviews for his performance in Stephen Crane's Civil War Classic, *The Red Badge of Courage*, directed by John Huston.

When he returned to civilian life, Audie suffered from what today is known as Post Traumatic Stress Disorder. He slept with a loaded pistol under his pillow and became addicted to sleeping pills.

Although he had financial problems prior to his death in 1971, Audie refused to appear in alcohol and cigarette commercials, as he thought such action would convey the wrong message to young people.

He is buried in Arlington Nation Cemetery where his grave site is the second most visited after President John F. Kennedy's. Prater is buried at the National Cemetery in Chattanooga.

A Democrat in the Brock Family
William Emerson Brock

William "Bill" Emerson Brock, III's defeat of favored Democrat Wilkes T. Thrasher Jr. in the 1962 Third Congressional District race in Tennessee started the transformation of said district into a Republican stronghold which continues to this day.

Except for Marilyn Lloyd's upset defeat of incumbent Lamar Baker in 1974 during the Watergate scandal in the Richard Nixon administration in Washington, the Third District seat has been held by a Republican. After Lloyd retired in 1994, Zach Wamp and Chuck Fleischman have represented the District as our Congressmen.

However Bill Brock was not the first member of his family from Chattanooga to hold public office in Washington. His grandfather, William E. Brock, Sr. served as a United States Senator from 1929-1931 as a member of the Democratic Party. In 1929, Brock Sr. was appointed by Tennessee Governor Henry Horton to fill the vacancy in the Senate caused by the death of Senator Lawrence D. Tyson in September, 1929. Although he was reelected in November, 1930, Brock chose not to run again in 1931 and left office on March 4th, 1931.

William E. Brock, Sr. was born in Mocksville, North Carolina, on March 14th, 1872. Upon the death of his father when the young Brock was only in the fourth grade, he took over the operation of the family farm and dropped out of school to help support his mother and brothers and sisters. He moved to Chattanooga in his twenties and became a merchant. Using a borrowed sum of four thousand dollars ($4,000.00) he originally became a candy wholesaler and eventually became a manufacturer of confections. Brock Candy grew into one of the largest candy companies in the country.

As his company grew, he became a leader in not only the business community but also in civic and other public activities. Brock Sr. and his wife, Miriam Acree, both were also deeply involved in the religious life of Chattanooga. She was instrumental in the creation of several churches in the African American community. A devout Methodist, he for many years taught the largest men's Bible class at Trinity Methodist Church. He also worked with Dr. J.P. McCallie to introduce Bible teaching as part of the curriculum in the Chattanooga public school system.

Brock's appointment to the United States Senate in 1929 involved several unusual political events. Cordell Hull of Pickett County had continuously served as a Congressman from middle Tennessee from 1906 to 1931 except for a two year gap. In an unsuspected move, Hull in 1929 announced he was going to run for the United States Senate seat, prior to Brock's confirmation by the Senate. Senator Lawrence D. Tyson had died in office on August 24th, 1929, creating a vacancy in Tennessee's delegation. Governor Henry Horton had initially offered the position to Luke Lea, publisher of *Nashville Tennessean* newspaper. Lea had been eliminated in the Democratic Primary that year and chose to decline the senatorial appointment from Governor Horton, who then offered it to William E. Brock, Sr.

Brock's getting the appointment did not deter Cordell Hull from announcing his candidacy for the seat in 1931. Whatever his reasons, Brock chose only to remain in office from September 2nd, 1929, through March 4th, 1931. Hull only served two years as a junior Senator from Tennessee and in 1933 was selected by President Franklin D. Roosevelt to be appointed Secretary of State. He would become the longest serving government official in that position in America history (1933-1944).

Although William Emerson Brock, Sr. had turned over the operation of Brock Candy Company to his son William E. Brock, Jr. after he became a member of Congress, he remained heavily involved in the operation of the company and community activities until his death on August 5th, 1950.

William E. Brock

Carey Estes Kefauver
Chattanooga's Congressman and Senator

Much is known of Carey Estes Kefauver's career as a Congressman, Senator and aspiring presidential candidate, but his ties to Chattanooga likewise were an important part of his life. Kefauver was born July 26th, 1903 in Madisonville, Tennessee. After graduating from University of Tennessee at Knoxville in 1924 and Yale University Law School in New Haven, Connecticut, he entered the practice of law in Chattanooga in 1927.

Kefauver became associated with Cooke, Swaney, and Cooke, which was the oldest local law firm in existence at that time. Although he had family connections with the Cooke firm, he subsequently moved to the firm headed by attorney J.B. Sizer, and it was renamed Sizer, Chambliss and Kefauver, which was the forerunner of the present leading Chattanooga firm of Chambliss, Bahner and Stophel.

Kefauver immediately became recognized as a talented lawyer and also engaged in civic activities and politics.

In 1928-1931 he served as a member of the Board of Governors, Secretary and Vice President of the Chattanooga Bar Association.

In 1938 he ran for the Senate but was defeated in the Democratic Primary by fellow attorney, Joe Bean, uncle of present City of Chattanooga Judge Russell Bean. However his excellent showing in the narrow defeat resulted in Kefauver's being appointed Commissioner of Finance and Taxation by Tennessee Governor Prentice Cooper.

Kefauver was always heavily involved in community activities, and in 1937 he was chosen by the Chattanooga Junior Chamber of Commerce as "Young Man of the Year."

While a practicing attorney Kefauver's law firm did mostly corporate work for many of the legal business corporations in the area. The firm also represented the *Chattanooga News* which was a pro-union newspaper. However when Kefauver made an anti-union speech to a local civic club, it resulted in scalding editorials by the newspaper.

He later met with union officials and acknowledged that he was generally unaware of the "economic, political and human problems which led to the beginning and growth of the labor movement."

From that point until his untimely death in 1963, Kefauver was described as a "good listener" to both management and labor positions. While he never gave either side 100% support, both sides often felt they could talk to him, ever when he would disagree with their positions.

When Congressman Sam McReynolds of Tennessee's Third Congressional District died in 1939, Kefauver was selected to succeed him in the House of Representatives.

As a Congressman Kefauver supported much of President Franklin Delano Roosevelt's "New Deal" legislation including the controversial Tennessee Valley Authority Act.

As Kefauver's national prominence rose, he became an avowed enemy of the Democratic Party head in Tennessee, Edward Hull "Boss" Crump of Memphis.

In 1948 Kefauver sought and won the Democratic nomination for the United States Senate seat against Republican B. Carroll Reece of east Tennessee.

In face of strong accusations from the Crump political machine calling Kefauver a liberal outside the political beliefs of Tennesseans "with the stealth of a raccoon," Kefauver turned the remark around to his advantage. Donning a Davy Crockett style coon skin cap, Kefauver went on television and remarked, "I may be a pet coon, but I am not boss Crump's pet coon!"

Kefauver was admired and respected by many less liberal leaders in the state because of his integrity and willingness to boldly defend himself against Crump and his supporters which ultimately led to the collapse of that political machine.

Kefauver's political star continued to rise and he became a national figure. As head of the Kefauver Committee it was publicly disclosed on national television for the first time the workings of the Mafia and organized crime in America.

Other controversial stands while representing Tennessee included the enactment of the Kefauver-Harris Drug Act. It strengthened the power of the United States Food and Drug Administration to regulate the pharmaceutical industries ability to impose excess profits that the drug companies were making at the expense of consumers. Said legislation faced strong opposition with the American Medical Association and physicians, as well as the drug industry. However, the revelation of an epidemic of deformed babies whose mothers had taken the drug thalidomide during pregnancy led to the passage of stronger regulations in 1961, an agency which continues today as the Federal Drug Administration.

Along with fellow Tennessean, Albert Gore, Sr., and Senate majority leader, Lyndon B. Johnson of Texas, Kefauver was one of the three Senators to vote against the Southern Manifesto of 1948, designed to impede the removal of segregation in America.

Though unpopular throughout the South for his liberal stances, Kefauver, with his highly publicized attacks on subjects such as pornography and the use of pinup girls in magazines, remained in the national political picture.

In 1952 he ran for the Democratic Party nomination for President. Although he won several primaries he incurred the private wrath of President Harry S. Truman, and the nomination eventually went to one-term Governor, Adali Stephenson of Illinois.

After President Dwight D. Eisenhower easily defeated the Democratic ticket of Stephenson and Senator John Sparkman of Alabama, Kefauver tried again for the presidency nomination in 1956.

Although he won several early primaries, his campaign once again ran out of steam, and Governor Stephenson was once again nominated to take on the Eisenhower-Richard M. Nixon Republican team.

In a surprise political move, Stephenson in an attempt to unify the Democratic Party, decided to let the delegates to the convention choose his vice presidential running mate. In a heated contest with Senator John F. Kennedy of Massachusetts, Kefauver was eventually chosen.

The Democratic ticket lost the 1956 election to Eisenhower-Nixon by an even larger margin than in 1952.

Although Kefauver was considered to be the favorite candidate to head the Democratic ticket in 1960, the nomination went to Senator Kennedy, who, with Senator Lyndon B. Johnson, defeated the Richard Nixon-Senator Henry Cabot Lodge Republican candidates in one of the closest and most controversial presidential contests in American history.

Kefauver had announced in 1959 that he would not enter the presidential race in 1960 and sought re-election to his Tennessee Senate seat for a third term in 1960. Despite his stand against segregation, he was successful in handily winning the nomination in the Democratic Primary. Although few Tennesseans would publicly support him in the General Election, he defeated his Republican opponent, A. Brady Frazier, winning 72% of the vote.

Kefauver's term of service began in 1959, when he gave up his presidential ambitions until his sudden death from a heart attack in 1963, has been described by several political historians as his most productive period of service in Congress. Kefauver proudly claimed that his efforts in getting the Kefauver-Harris Drug Control Act was his "finest achievement" in consumer protection litigation. It established controls on the drug companies for the benefit of the sick citizens that used their products.

On the seventy-fifth anniversary of the Chattanooga Bar Association, attorney Clarence Kolwyck described Kefauver as a man "seldom free of controversy" who did not know the meaning of compromise, and, "Like him or not, the Chattanooga Bar Association should claim Estes Kefauver with pride."

Liberal Democrat C. Estes Kefauver and conservative Republican William Emerson Brock, III, both commendably served the Third Congressional District and the United States Senate with distinction as Chattanooga's representatives in the years between 1948 and 1977. Although their political positions differed on many issues, their service to our state and nation are important parts of the political history of Chattanooga and Tennessee.

Estes Kefauver in coon-skin cap, 1958

Nathan Lynn Bachman
Beloved Tennessee Senator

Nathan L. Bachman was a highly respected judicial officer from Chattanooga on both state and national levels.

He was born August 2, 1878. After attending the University of Chattanooga and the University of Virginia he received a law degree from the latter in 1903 and returned to Chattanooga to enter the practice of law.

Bachman was fortunate to be a member of a well-known and prominent family and was appointed City Attorney in Chattanooga in 1906.

He entered politics and in 1912 was elected Circuit Court Judge. In 1918 after serving only six years, he was elected to the Tennessee Supreme Court.

In 1923 he resigned from the position to become a candidate for the United States Senate in 1924.

Incumbent Senator John Knight Shields, of Bean Station and Knoxville, had incurred the opposition of President Woodrow Wilson because of Shields' reluctance to support America's participation in the League of Nations, Wilson's favorite project and the ill-fated predecessor to NATO. Shortly before his death, President Wilson had attacked Shields in a letter to Tennesseans. Due to the degree of the president's popularity in the state, the letter adversely affected Shields chances for re-election.

In 1924 Bachman and General Lawrence D. Tyson, a World War I hero and former Speaker of the Tennessee House of Representatives, opposed Shields in the Democratic Primary.

Although Tyson won the nomination in a campaign where he spent a substantiated sum of money for the times, Bachman finished a credible third. He received a large number of votes in Hamilton County, greatly exceeding that of the other two candidates combined.

Tyson's victory in the 1924 race was followed by his death in 1929. Chattanoogan William E. Brock, Sr., father of future Republican Congressman and Senator Bill Brock, was appointed to fill the vacancy. Brock chose not to seek reelection in 1930 due to the early announcement that popular Congressman Cordell Hull was going to seek the office. Hull was elected in 1930 but only served two years in the Senate, as he was appointed to be Secretary of State by President Franklin D. Roosevelt.

Bachman had returned to a lucrative practice of law in Chattanooga and had gotten married to Pearl Duke, a member of the wealthy Duke family in North Carolina that founded Duke University.

On February 28, 1933, Bachman was selected from a large number of prospective senatorial candidates by Governor Hill McAllister to fill the position vacated by Hull in the United States Senate.

From historical accounts, Bachman enjoyed the work and companionship in the Senate and was an effective legislator, developing a reputation of being a good storyteller who was popular as a junior senator to Senator Kenneth McKellar of Memphis.

Congressman (and future governor) Gordon Browning of Huntington, Tennessee, was ambitious to become a Senator and ran against Bachman in the Democratic Primary in 1934.

Nathan Lynn Bachman

With the support of Senator McKellar, Bachman defeated Browning by 40,000 votes. With his strong showing, he discouraged prospective opponents in 1936 when he was re-elected for a full six-year senate term. Unfortunately Bachman would only serve three months when he suffered a heart attack and died in Washington, D.C. on April 23, 1937, at the age of fifty-eight.

A ten member delegation of Congressional representatives headed by Senator McKellar and including future president Harry S. Truman, attended a large funeral conducted in Chattanooga when 136 individuals from all over the state served as honorary pallbearers.

In recognition of Nathan Bachman's popularity in the area, an elementary school in the community of Signal Mountain, where he lived prior to his death, was named for him.

He was a well-known and popular legal, judicial and political leader who unfortunately died at an early age as his political star was ascending.

Thomas Jefferson Anderson
Baylor School's Presidential Candidate

In 1972 and 1976, the Baylor School had a 1930 graduate on the ballot in the presidential races.

Thomas "Tom" Jefferson Anderson was nominated as a vice presidential candidate in 1972 as the running mate of Congressman John Schmitz of California for the American Independent Party (A.I.P.). Both Schmitz and Anderson were strong right-wing conservatives and members of the John Birch Society.

Tom Anderson

The A.I.P. had previously been formed in 1968 to create a third party to support Alabama Governor George C. Wallace and retired Air Force General Curtis LeMay. These candidates received 13.5% of the popular vote and 46 electoral college votes.

In 1976 the name of the party had been changed to the American Party, and Anderson was the presidential nominee with Rufus Shackelford, a millionaire tomato grower from Wauchula, Florida, as the vice-president candidate. Anderson always credited Baylor for advancing his career. A mediocre student in high school in Nashville, his father agreed to transfer Tom to the Chattanooga preparatory school on the Tennessee River.

Anderson has stated, "My dear daddy sent me to a good school, Baylor in Chattanooga, Tennessee, where a degree from it meant something!" His Baylor degree got him into Vanderbilt University in Nashville where he excelled in track and tennis and also served as business editor of the school yearbook, *The Commodore*, and he was a member of the student newspaper staff. He is credited with delivering more than 1,500 speeches between 1947-1994.

Following a tenure in the security market for several Nashville brokerage firms and service in the United States Navy in World War II, he purchased *The Arkansas Farmer,* which was the forerunner of sixteen regional farm magazines he acquired as part of a Nashville based publication conglomerate.

Anderson received his greatest recognition as the author of his regular newspaper column, "Straight Talk." A conservative oriented publication, it was included in more than 375 local newspapers. "Straight Talk" was also the title of a weekly national radio show as a voice for conservative politics.

He remained active in the John Birch Society and was a popular radio and television orator. Displaying a great sense of humor, he was often referred to as "a modern-day Will Rodgers." Other critics referred to him as the barefoot wit of the John Birch Society.

He was recognized by both conservative and national patriotic groups and was presented the Liberty Award of the Congress of Freedom and a Freedom Award from the Freedom Foundation at Valley Forge.

Anderson remained a staunch conservative until his death on August 30, 2002, at the age of ninety-one and is interred at the Mount Hope Cemetery at Franklin in Williamson County, Tennessee.

Tennessee's Unholy Trinity
Cummings, Beasley and Haynes

Before the landmark United States Supreme Court decision of Baker v. Carr, 369 U.S. 186 (1962) establishing the "one man, one vote" standard for legislative districting, three rural Tennessee legislators, Jim Cummings of Woodbury, I.D. Beasley of Carthage, and Walter (Pete) Haynes of Winchester, kept the legislature under the control of the rural interests of the state at the expense of the larger cities such as Memphis, Nashville, Knoxville and Chattanooga. They would often be joined in their bloc by Paul (Stump Daddy) Graham of South Pittsburg.

Mr. **Jim Cummings** was the leader of the influential trio that held the metropolitan areas captive and was subsequently given the honorary title of "Dean of the Legislature." He also was referred to as "The Last Man of the Four Dollar Day Meal," because during his legislative service Tennessee General Assembly members were paid no salary and were allotted only $4.00/day in expense money. He was born on November 8, 1890, in Cannon County, Tennessee, and initially became a school teacher, circuit court clerk, and publisher of the *Cannon Carrier* from 1916-1918, prior to becoming a clerk in the State Comptroller's Office in Nashville. He used his position to attend the YMCA night law school where he was admitted to the bar in 1922. He then attended Cumberland University in Lebanon, Tennessee, where he earned his diploma in 1923.

After an unsuccessful venture in the Florida postwar boom, Cummings returned to Woodbury and entered the practice of law. A successful law practice allowed him to gain enough public recognition to run and win a seat in the State Senate in 1929. He would continue to serve in the General Assembly as either a senator or representative for over forty years and never lost an election.

The era of the control of Memphis by Edward H. Crump's (the Red Snapper) political machine had a direct conflict with Cummings and his other colleagues representing the rural communities in the state. The power of the Cummings bloc continued beyond the demise of the Crump machine in the 1950's, and the big cities would remain subservient to rural counties until the Baker v. Carr decision in 1962. Cummings once summed up the philosophy of the colleagues as follows, "Raise the money in the cities and spend it in the county!" As a result, tiny Cannon County represented by Cummings had more employees on the State payroll than did the much larger city of Knoxville.

I.D. Beasley of Carthage was another member of Cummings' rural bloc in the legislature. A short, heavyset man, he possessed the unique quality of being able to duplicate the voice of any man or woman. He often used this unusual characteristic to either play practical jokes or to turn politicians around on any issue that might pertain to the interest of the rural bloc in the legislature. During the legislative session in Nashville, he roomed with Jim Cummings. Both of them were well known for getting their meals and free whiskey from lobbyists that were known as "a golden goose." Beasley was not only part of the Cummings-Beasley-Haynes rural voting bloc. He was also fondly thought of by those who knew him in Nashville as a legislator.

Beasley created a lifelong friendship with Jim Farley, chairman of the national Democratic Party and Franklin D. Roosevelt's chief political operative. The friendship arose out of a joke Beasley played on Farley by mimicking Cordell Hull, Secretary of State. As a result, Farley appointed I.D. to be a sergeant at arms, who accompanied Cummings as a non-delegate to each National Democratic Party Convention and allegedly received more privileges and benefits than the actual delegates themselves.

Beasley's ability to mimic everyone created a lot of humor and chaos with many legislators who might not have complied with the laws and rules pertaining to Prohibition and morality.

The third member of the Unholy Trinity was **Pete Haynes**, a representative from Franklin County who also was a successful trial lawyer who served five terms as speaker of either the Tennessee House of Representatives or Senate. As a speaker, he held life or death power over legislation as he appointed committee chairmen and decided which legislation would come to a vote. The Unholy Trinity's battles with Boss Crump are part of the political history of the Volunteer State.

Haynes also possessed the talent of being a master forger of written documents. This talent came into use when the trio needed a vote or two. Using personal notepads bearing the Governor's name that were stolen from his office, the trio would have Haynes forge a note asking the representative or senator to come to the Governors Office immediately. While the unsuspecting legislator was at the Executives Office, the bill in question would be brought to the floor, and in his absence would either pass or fail without his vote.

Former Governor Buford Ellington was quoted as saying, "If these three decided to kill you on a particular bill they could.....It was as simple as that....When the wanted something, they got it by hook or crook.....Whenever Jim or I.D. or Pete came to my office, the first thing I would do was hide my personal notepads."

Using tactics that were both humorous and illegal, or least unethical, this trio of rural legislators had a lasting and unbreakable effect upon the Tennessee General Assembly prior to the Baker v. Carr decision.

Ironically, Chattanooga attorney Ray Brock, in the defense of controversial Hamilton County Judge Raulston Schoolfield in his impeachment trial in 1958 by the Tennessee General Assembly, had raised the same re-apportionment issue ,claiming that the legislative composition was illegal and lacked jurisdiction to try the jurist. The issue was never decided by the legislative body, and Schoolfield was impeached and subsequently disbarred by the Tennessee Supreme Court.

According to sources, Brock begged Schoolfield to allow him to appeal the disbarment ruling to the United States Supreme Court. Although the re-apportionment issue had been dropped in the impeachment trial and not raised in the disbarment case, if it had been pursued, the Schoolfield case may have become the historical legal authority rather than Baker v. Carr.

The antics of Cummings, Haynes, and Beasley would probably be unacceptable today, but their paralyzing hold on state government greatly benefited their rural constituents. Two areas they vigorously opposed were truck weight limits and morality bills.

Cummings served 36 years in the Tennessee General Assembly and never lost a race. Pete Haynes acquired a reputation in Franklin County and the state as a successful trial lawyer and allegedly only lost one capital murder case out of 400 that resulted in a client being executed. I.D. Beasley was a short, overweight colleague who was the court jester of the trio. His ability to mimic political figures was often used to mislead legislators into voting for the side of the Unholy Trinity.

It was a different time, and many of their power-wielding tactics of those days would not be allowed today, but it provided a colorful chapter into the political history of the State of Tennessee.

Two-thirds of the Unholy Trinity with, left to right, Education Commissioner J. M. Smith, Representative McAllen Foutch, Jim Cummings and I. D Beasley

Pete Haynes entertains President Kennedy and the First Lady. Both photos courtesyof *The Tennessean.*

Pioneer Women Attorneys in Southeast Tennessee

When former Chief Justice A.B. Neil of the Tennessee Supreme Court wrote his autobiography, *My Great World* in 1964, he noted that he had, "Never expected to see the day when females would be lawyers!"

Although the records of the Chattanooga College of Law indicate that several women attended the school in the 1920's-1930's, few, if any, actually engaged in the practice of law in southeast Tennessee. However, the present legal climate is much friendlier towards females. Of the 1,240 attorneys licensed to practice law in Hamilton County, 357 are women. Also the Tennessee Supreme Court headed by Chief Justice Sharon Lee includes Justice Holly Kirby and Justice Cornelia Clark.

Women serve as judges in all courts of record in both the state and federal systems, and many more engage in every aspect of the legal profession. Five of the women mentioned below were pioneers in certain areas of the law in the 1930's to the present.

Marguerite Lanham graduated from Chattanooga High School and attended the University of Chattanooga prior to graduating from the Chattanooga College of Law in 1935. She was subsequently admitted to the practice of law in 1936.

She distinguished herself by being the first woman to try a criminal case in Hamilton County before Judge Charles Lusk, was the second woman to be admitted to the Tennessee Supreme Court, and was the first female attorney to be accepted to practice in the United States District Court by Judge Leslie Darr in Chattanooga in 1939. She practiced until 1989 with her nephew by marriage, Alf R. (Tony) O'Rear.

She ran unsuccessfully for General Sessions Court judge in 1958 and took great issue with a newspaper editorial that a woman should not be "exposed" to some things that had to be aired in open court. Her response to the attack was to assert, "A trained legal mind has no sex." She died at the age of eighty-eight.

Opal Scanland graduated from the University of Tennessee at Knoxville and the Chattanooga College of Law in 1958. She always had a special interest in juvenile law and worked in the Hamilton County Juvenile Court as a probation officer. Opal also served as a special judge in that court during the medical disability of juvenile Judge Leo Britt. She died suddenly in 1989 at the age of seventy-one.

Selma (Sunny) Cash Paty graduated from Cumberland Law School in Lebanon, Tennessee, with two degrees in law in 1947. She was the first woman elected as president of the Chattanooga Bar Association and was the only woman selected in the initial class of the Chattanooga Bar Foundation. Active in state legal organizations, she served on the Board of Governors of both the Tennessee Bar Association and the Tennessee Trial Lawyers Association. She was the unsuccessful plaintiff in the landmark decision of *Paty v. McDaniel* in the United States Supreme Court. The decision struck down the provision in the Tennessee constitution which prohibited ministers from running for political office. She died May 1, 2016.

Claude Swafford graduated from the University of Tennessee at Knoxville College of Law and had been engaged in the legal profession for seventy years when she died in March, 25, 2016. A resident of Marion County where she practiced with her husband, Howard, and son, Graham, she always had a special interest in education. During the 1970's, she fought unsuccessfully to consolidate the school systems in Marion County and was an outspoken advocate for said cause.

Ardena Garth has been the youngest pioneer for women's rights in law. She served as the first female African American public defender in Hamilton County from 1996-2014. A graduate of Ooltewah High School and the University of Kansas Law School, she was defeated for re-election in her last race.

These five women helped open the doors for the many female attorneys that now engage in the practice of law in our courts as judges, prosecutors, defense counsel, associates and partners in large law firms and sole practitioners.

They, along with others, helped to open up the legal profession to women wanting to be a part of the group of lawyers serving clients in Hamilton County and southeast Tennessee.

Byron De La Beckweth – Signal Mountain's Infamous Resident (1920-2001)

In a wooded area between the W Road and Taft Highwa on Albion Drive, lies the former residence of Byron De La Beckwith, convicted killer of National Association for the Advancement of Colored People (NAAC) Mississippi field secretary, Medgar Evans, on June 12, 1963, in Jackson, Mississippi.

De La Beckweth was born on November 9, 1920, in Colusa, California, and at the age of six moved to Greenwood, Mississippi, where his mother died of lung cancer when he was twelve. After an unsuccessful college career, De La Beckwith enlisted in the United States Marine Corps in 1942 and was assigned to duty as a machine gunner in the Pacific in World War II. He participated in the Battle of Guadalcanal and was wounded in the stomach during the battle of Tarawa. He received a Purple Heart and was honorably discharged in 1945.

When he returned to Greenwood after the war, he married his first wife, Mary Louise Williams (1946 – 1960) and became a member of the Ku Klux Klan and the segregationist White Citizens Council that was formed after the ruling in 1954's decision of Brown v. Board of Education. The Council used a variety of economic tactics "to suppress black activism and sustain segregation" by boycotting black business, denying loans and credit to blacks, and other non-violent actions.

However, De La Beckwith, as a white supremacist and Klansman, did not believe that the violent (Klan) and non-violent (Citizen's Council) efforts were successful enough in stopping integration of the races. On June 12, 1963, he shot Medgar Evers as he was getting out of his car at his home. He was shot in the back by an assassin from across the street.

Although De La Beckwith was arrested for the crime, two all-white male juries could not reach a verdict in 1964. The White Citizens Council had paid for his legal defense in both trials.

De La Beckwith moved to a wooded residence on Signal Mountain and lived a rather obscure existence with his second wife, Thelma Neff (1981 – 2001) until Medgar Evers' widow, Myrlie Evers Williams, pushed for another trial after a newspaper investigation revealed proof that a state agency committed jury tampering in the 1964 trials.

Times had changed in the 1990s, and a new and ambitious prosecutor, Bobby DeLaughter, brought a third indictment before the grand jury in Jackson charging De La Beckwith once again in 1990.

He was extradited back to Mississippi after several unsuccessful years of legal maneuvers by his appointed defense counsel. (See De La Beckwith v. State 707 So.2d 547 [Miss 1997] cert, denied 525 U.S. 880) he went to trial over objections by his lawyer to dismiss the charges on grounds of denial of a speedy trial, due process of law, and protection from double jeopardy. The Mississippi Supreme Court, by a vote of 4-3, hence denied the motion to dismiss.

In January the third trial started, and the physical evidence was the same except De La Beckwith had made several admissions before witnesses that he had shot Evers and stated, "Killing that N_ _ _ _ _ gave me no more inner discomfort than our wives endure when they gave birth to our children".

Or

"When I go to Hades I am going to raise hell all over Hades till I get to the white section; for the next 15 years, we here in Mississippi are going to have to do a lot of shooting to protect or wives and children from a lot of bad N_ _ _ _ _ _ _".

A mixed jury of black and white jurors found De La Beckwith guilty of first degree murder without the possibility of parole and sentenced him to life imprisonment at Central Mississippi Correctional Center.

On January 21, 2001, at the age of 80, De La Beckwith died at the University of Mississippi Medical Center in Jackson, Mississippi, after suffering from heart disease, high blood pressure and other ailments.

He was interred at Chattanooga Memorial Park also known as White Oak Cemetery in the community of White Oak, Tennessee. Many publications have been written about the murder of Medgar Evers. The feature film, "Ghosts of Mississippi" (1966) tells the story of the murder and 1994 trial. James Woods' performance of De La Beckwith was nominated for an Academy Award.

Bobby DeLaughter, who was once being considered for a Federal Judgeship, was suspended from the practice of law by the Mississippi

Byron De La Beckweth

Supreme Court on allegations of bribery and judicial corruption while a state judge.

On July 30, 2009, he pled guilty to one federal obstruction of justice charge and was sentenced to 18 months in the federal prison at McCreary, Kentucky. Said charge was linked to the criminal investigation of tort, asbestos & tobacco litigation lawyer, Richard "Dickie" Scruggs. Scruggs would be sentenced to jail for 5 years and was disbarred from the practice of law.

When "Lucky Lindy" Landed in Chattanooga

Prior to the opening of Lovell Field in 1930 as Chattanooga's primary airport, two grass strips handled air traffic in our city. Brainerd Field was located west of the Brainerd Golf Course, and Marr Field was located near the south end of Amnicola Highway between the railroad and Dodson Avenue north of Glass Street in East Chattanooga.

Marr Field was named after Walter Marr who was a successful executive in the automobile industry. Marr was employed at the Buick Motor Company and was its chief engineer. He subsequently moved to Signal Mountain and constructed an elaborate mansion which exists to this day after extreme renovations by the present owners. Marr developed interests in bicycles, boats, engines and finally automobiles which resulted in his having financial success.

Marr had visited the Chattanooga area in 1914, and the cool mountain breezes on Signal Mountain convinced him and his family to establish a residence in a cottage near the Signal Mountain Inn. Ultimately they would erect an elegant home called Marrcrest. The residence was built of fireproof materials involving poured concrete and marble floors.

The Chattanooga Chamber of Commerce was the motivating organization in the creation of Marr Field in the 1910's. An aviation committee of the Chamber of Commerce would ultimately obtain leases on the property where the airport was to be located in 1919.

Marr had become very interested in the development of aviation and worked closely with the Chamber and actively supported its efforts in building the East Chattanooga landing strip. He even assisted the Hamilton County Road Department in its clearance of the land for the airport in November, 1919. As a result, Marr Field was named in his honor.

The airfield was scheduled to be dedicated on Thanksgiving Day in 1919, but inclement weather delayed the ceremony until December 5, 1919.

Ironically the military officer in charge of the Army aviation in the Southeast arrived at Marr Field accompanied by John Lovell, chairman of the Chattanooga Chamber of Commerce as a passenger. Although the Army official praised Marr Field as being a leading aviation facility of the South, it quickly developed that the location of the airstrip was hazardous to planes flying in the area due to its close proximity to Missionary Ridge and the railroad property.

Numerous airplane crashes occurred, and two fatal accidents took place. One in March, 1927, resulted in the death of a single pilot and four other passengers. In a tragedy in December, 1928, an airmail plane operated by Interstate Airlines crashed.

As a result, in 1929 plans were enacted to erect another airport, and in 1930 Lovell Field opened in its present location along South Chickamauga Creek. By 1935 Marr Field had ceased to exist as a commercial aviation facility.

However, prior to its demise, Marr Field was visited by the most famous aviator in the country during this era. Charles A. Lindbergh landed there on October 5, 1927 in his famous aircraft, Spirit of St. Louis.

In May, 1927, Lindbergh successfully crossed the Atlantic Ocean from New York and landed at Orly Airport in Paris, France, winning the $25,000.00 prize under the challenge created by New York hotelier, Raymond Orteig.

As a result of the feat, Lindbergh was asked by Congressman Edward B. Almon of Tuscumbia, Alabama, to fly over several key cities in his congressional district. Lindbergh's flight were part of a three-month nationwide tour sponsored by millionaire Daniel Guggenheim to raise awareness and popular interest in the new industry of commercial aviation.

On October 5, 1927, Lindbergh flew over many cities in the Southeast and dropped several letters of greeting out of his plane as he flew over them. At 10:30 a.m., he landed at Marr Field in Chattanooga and "was given the greatest celebration since the days of the world war."

"Lucky Lindy" then traveled to Alabama and Mississippi on the next legs of his nationwide Guggenheim tour.

Marr Field had reached the zenith of its existence with the Lindberg landing. With the development of Lovell Field, it would fall out of favor and failed to exist around 1935.

The Other Plane & Pilot at Marr Field
Phillip R. Love, October 5, 1927

The stop of Charles Lindbergh at Chattanooga's Marr Field in East Chattanooga, north of Glass Street, on October 5, 1927, as part of his international tour of America, Canada, Mexico, and the Caribbean are well documented in the literature and history books.

Much less is known of the pilot and aircraft that accompanied Lindbergh and preceded him on each of the approximate eighty city stops in the United States and Canada and the fifteen countries south of the border. The flights started on July 20, 1927, and ended in Havana, Cuba, on February 13, 1928.

The trip financed by the Daniel Guggenheim Fund included an escort aircraft that would carry one pilot and four passengers.

The trip by the Spirit of St. Louis was designed to promote development of aviation with the Department of Commerce of the United States Government as a sponsor.

The aircraft chosen to land ahead of Lindbergh at each of the designated stops on the itinerary was a Fairchild FC-2 (Fairchild Cabin No. 2) and was powered by a Wright J-15 radial engine producing 220 horsepower, which was the same type and model in the Spirit of St. Louis.

The aircraft had a fuel capacity of seventy-five gallons and could cruise at 103 miles/hour. The plane could carry a gross weight of 3,225 pounds, which would include spare parts and tools, as well as other baggage, cameras, and a crew of four that might be needed to service it and Lindbergh's plane throughout the lengthy trip. It had a unique feature that allowed its wings to be folded back in order that it could be stored overnight in smaller areas since the Spirit did not have the same flexibility.

The Fairchild was piloted by Phillip R. Love. Its crew consisted of D.E. Keyhoe, who served as manager of the tour, and C.C. Maidmont, who was an experienced aviation mechanic and who performed any necessary repairs on either of the planes.

The literature about the Fairchild has conflicts about its description. Some articles describe it as a "red" monoplane while others claim the fuselage was painted black as well as markings on the wing, fins, and rudder. Other parts of the wings and tail group were painted orange. It had been described as, "The one-ton truck of the air, a jack-of-all-trades aircraft." Unlike the Spirit it was of all metal construction. Its fuel capacity was much less than the Spirit. Nevertheless it was a powerful aircraft that performed well throughout the entire tour.

Phillip R. Love was a longtime friend of Charles Lindbergh and had served with him in the Army and as pilots in the infant United States Mail Service. Lindbergh specifically requested that Love be selected as pilot of the escort Fairchild plane owned by the Department of Commerce.

As a testament of Lindbergh's confidence in Love, he was only one of two pilots that were authorized by Lindbergh to fly the Spirit without him being present. The event was a ten minute flight over Louisville, Kentucky.

The standard procedure was that Love would take off thirty minutes prior to Lindbergh and would land before the Spirit in order to prepare the welcoming committee for his arrival.

Lindbergh would be participating in the festivities at each location by giving a speech promoting aviation and accepting one of the thousands of gifts or commemorative scrolls. Meanwhile Love and Maidmont would check the mechanical condition of each plane and prepare them for the next leg of the trip.

Phil Love achieved the rank of Colonel on the United States Army Air Corps and was killed in a plane crash on May 31, 1943, when his Douglas C-67 struck a mountain peak in Nevada while on a flight leg from Colorado Springs, Colorado, to Reno, Nevada.

Prior to his death he was an outspoken advocate of the development of aviation and spoke on the subject on many occasions.

On May 23, 1929,, he addressed a national aeronautical group in St. Louis and advised the body, "It is as necessary for a town or area to provide facilities and accept and adopt aviation now as it was for acceptance and adoption of the railroad three quarters a century ago!"

Phil Love was always considered by Charles Lindbergh as being a vital part of the successful completion of the post New York to Paris tour across America and other countries.

Jim T. Fitzgerald, Jr.
South Pittsburg's Sound Barrier Breaker
July 13, 1920-September 20, 1948

If it weren't for the performance of Captain Chuck Yeager being the first individual to break the sound barrier in 1947, South Pittsburg's James (Jim) Thomas Fitzgerald, Jr. would have gained such worldwide acclamation and fame. As the second aviator to accomplish such a feat, Jim has been relatively anonymous in spite of his many accomplishments in support of his country.

Jim Fitzgerald, Jr. was born in South Pittsburg, Tennessee, in 1920 and attended South Pittsburg High School. He graduated in 1938 and served as Vice-President of his senior class. He received an appointment to the United State Military Academy at West Point.

During his youth, Jim expressed an early interest in aviation, and one of his main interests was working on model airplanes. He won several statewide awards and trophies with his hobby and continued his interest in model planes throughout his life.

In preparation for trying to get an appointment to West Point, Jim enrolled in a six week training course at Fort Oglethorpe, Georgia, and won a fifty hour flying scholarship at a fixed based operation in Chattanooga operated by Harry Porter.

He was admitted to West Point on July 1, 1940, and after expressing an interest in aviation, he spend the next summer taking flying lessons in Bentonville, South Carolina, where he flew for the first time in the Army and received his wings as an Army aviator.

With the beginning of World War II, Jim received fighter training and was sent overseas to England in April, 1944, as part of the 78th Fighter group of the Eighth Air Force.

On his twenty-eighth combat mission, he was shot down and imprisoned at Stalag Luft III in Moosburg, Germany. Upon being liberated in April, 1945, he was awarded a Purple Heart and the Army Air Corps Air Medal.

Despite his numerous requests to be sent to the Pacific arena to fight the Japanese, he was assigned by the Pentagon to be a test pilot in the area of jet propelled aircraft, as the military recognized the need to develop the advanced aircraft of the defeated Germans.

In the fall of 1947, he was assigned to Wright Field in Dayton, Ohio, where research on the rocket plane, the Bell X-1 was being conducted.

After being transferred to Muroc Air Force Base in California he and Chuck Yeager were part of the team of pilots that flew the experimental Bell X-1.

In October 1947, Yeager was the first pilot to break the sound barrier in the X-1 after being dropped from a B-29 bomber "mother ship."

On his first flight, Jim also broke the record of flying higher and faster than anyone except Yeager. While his colleague received international fame as a part of aviation history, Fitzgerald did not consider his actions as being historical, and it was left to Chuck Yeager to make the announcement to Jim's family of his accomplishment. For his effort he was awarded another Air Medal.

Yeager in his autobiography, *Yeager,* paid tribute to Jim's flying ability as, "The best takeoff and landing pilot I ever saw."

In late 1948 upon returning to the base from the Cleveland, Ohio, air races, Jim crashed his T-33 aircraft. On landing, his wing hit the ground, the plane cartwheeled, and he sustained head injuries that resulted in his death eleven days later on September 20, 1948.

He was buried at the United State Military Academy at West Point with full military honors.

In the many tributes made in his memory, he was affectionately described for his modest and unassuming character as, "The guy from South Pittsburg who just happened to like to fly."

On October 29, 2006, Jim's hometown unveiled a Tennessee historic marker at the South Pittsburg American Legion Hall in his honor fifty-eight years after his death.

The marker was paid for by private donations and sponsored by the South Pittsburg Historic Preservation Society. It brought back many memories of one of Marion County's World War II heroes but who was best known for doing his duty in service of his country and disclaiming all credit for himself.

Joseph C. White
Chattanooga's Tuskegee Airman

The creation, history and fictionalization of the aviation entity Tuskegee Airman has been documented in military records, literature and film since the black United States Army Air Force unit was created prior to America's involvement in World War II, starting after the December 7, 1941, bombing of Pearl Harbor.

While much has been written about the Tuskegee Airmen's wartime accomplishments, their record had a much greater effect on the civil rights movement and steps toward the abolishment of segregation in the 1960's. The Airmen's wartime feats from 1943-1945 in Italy and Sicily in escorting bombers and the introduction of Jackie Robinson in major league baseball in 1947, plus pressure by civil rights groups were the major factors in President Harry S. Truman's signing Executive Order No. 9981, ending segregation of the races in the United States military in 1948.

Joseph C. White

James Mitchell, Gadsden, Alabama; Samuel Harper, Oliver Springs, Tennessee; and Joseph C. White, Chattanooga, were three of the young blacks that served in the Tuskegee Airmen from our area.

Joseph C. White (1927-2007) was born in Lawrence County, Alabama, but grew up in Chattanooga during the 1930's. He had developed an early interest in flying by building model planes and flying them. At an early age he became an Eagle Scout and in 1937 attended the first Boy Scout Jamboree in Washington, D.C., where he met Eleanor Roosevelt. He joined the Tuskegee Institute cadet aviation corps in the program that was created in 1941. He flew as fighter escort for the bombers for nine months and was proud of the fact his squadron did not lose a single bomber to Germany fighters during his term of service. This record was achieved by only one of the four squadrons in the 332 Fighter Group. It led to the erroneous myth that the Airmen did not have any bombers lost to enemy fighters during their term of service from their segregated base at Ramitelli Airfield in Italy under less than ideal living conditions. In reality, and later verified, Air Force records indicate that at least 25-27 bombers were lost to enemy fire, although this was a much lower downed-plane ratio that other escort fighter groups.

White was one of the fighter pilots in the 305 Squadron of the 332 Fighter Group that flew the Republic P-47 Thunderbolt and later the more powerful and legendary P-51 Mustang. They became known as the "Red Tails" or the "Red Tail Angels" because of their excellent records. The aircraft's rear tails and nose fuselages were painted red to distinguish the Airmen from other groups.

Nine hundred ninety-two pilots were trained at Tuskegee between 1941-1946. Sixty-eight pilots were killed in combat, and thirty-two were shot down and became prisoners of war. Of one hundred seventy-nine missions on which they escorted the bombers, they only lost the bigger ships to enemy fighters on seven occasions.

Three Distinguished Unit citations were awarded to the fighter groups as well as numerous individual Purple Hearts, Air Medals, Bronze Stars, and ninety-five Distinguished Flying Crosses.

With the benefit of the GI Bill post-war, Lieutenant White attended Fisk University in Nashville, the University of Tennessee, Walden University in Minneapolis, Minnesota, George Peabody College and the University of Minnesota. During his lifetime he earned a Bachelor of Science degree, two master's degrees and a doctor of philosophy.

A physicist and educator, he set up the state's first high school electronic program at Pearl High School in 1959 in Nashville. Doctor White also taught physics, mathematics, general science, electronics and chemistry in the public schools in Chattanooga and Nashville. During this time he also became an aviation instructor in radar and electronics.

After retirement from being a teacher, he frequently was asked to speak to groups to discuss his role in the Tuskegee Airmen and experiences as a Black aviator in World War II.

He died in 2007, is buried in Woodlawn Memorial Park and Mausoleum in Nashville, and was inducted posthumously into the Tennessee Aviation Hall of Fame on November 7, 2015, in, "Recognition of his extraordinary achievement and service to aviation for Tennessee, our nation and the world and for his service to our country."

Harry G. Porter
Daredevil & Aviator (1894-1988)

Most Chattanoogans remember Harry Porter as one of the pioneers in aviation in the Chattanooga area. In that capacity he achieved a lifetime of recognition as the principal supporter of Chattanooga aviation beginning in the 1920's. However, less is known of his daredevil feats as a motorcycle racer and stock car driver.

In 1921-1922, he raced at the Chattanooga Interstate Fair at the old horse racing track at Warner Park in his "No. 7" Dodge automobile. He completed the Five Mile Elimination Race in five minutes and forty-nine and a half seconds. In the twenty-five mile feature race, he finished second to future Lake Winnepesaukah developer and owner, Carl Dixon, with a time of thirty-four minutes and thirty-two seconds.

Porter had also previously raced motorcycles on his 1912 Indian model in the Chattanooga area during this period. He was a true daredevil and enjoyed the excitement of speed in any category.

Harry first flew a plane from Marr Field in East Chattanooga in 1923. Marr Field was located on the west side of Missionary Ridge and was susceptible to violent crosswinds that resulted in many aviation accidents. As a result, Lovell Field on the eastern side of the ridge was constructed at its present location in 1930. During this early stage of his aviation career, Harry participated in barnstorming and flying shows across the South.

He also performed air shows every Sunday and gave plane rides. Soon people began asking for flying lessons that turned into Porter Flight Service in 1931. In 1938, the Tennessee Bureau of Aeronautics started a free flight instruction program with Harry as the instructor. The program was a boost to aviation in every major Tennessee city. Also in 1938, the first Chattanooga Flyers Club was established with several private pilots holding ownership rights to a few planes that would be available for use at an hourly rate. By pooling their efforts, more pilots could fly at a lower individual cost.

The state's Civilian Pilot Trainee Program was started in 1942 and changed the name to "War Training Service." Porters Flight Service was employed to train pilots for military service. Student pilots would attend classes in the morning at the University of Chattanooga and take flight instruction at Lovell Field in the afternoon under Porters supervision.

The program continued until 1944, and over 800 pilots obtained the primary training that would qualify them for the Army Air Corps flight program.

On March 26, 2003, eighty-two-year-old native of Soddy, James Thomas McClure, gave an interview in the Veterans History Project that vividly described his aviation training with Harry Porter.

Harry Porter, flight instructor

He would later convert that training into a career as an Army Air Corps instructor and Trans World Airways (TWA) pilot for twenty-eight years. He was highly complementary of the flight instruction that he received from Harry Porter and Buck Frame at Lovell Field.

In a 1987 interview with Porter, he recalls the two times he met famed aviator Charles Lindbergh. He first met the "Lone Eagle" in Americus, Georgia, at a government flight school in the early 1920's and described him as, "Just an average guy." Porter's second meeting with Lindbergh was on his 1927 stop in Chattanooga following his celebration tour after his historic New York to Paris flight.

Porter had a sixty-four year career in all aspects of aviation. In 1967 he sold his business to another fixed base operation, Hangar One, but remained a full-time consultant until his death in 1988. In 1974 he was given the Amelia Earhart Award by the 99's, an international women's flying organization, in recognition of his 80th birthday.

When he flew a plane at the age of ninety, he was considered the oldest active pilot in the country. In the 80's, the new air traffic control tower was named the Harry Porter Tower in his honor.

He served as a sergeant in World War I in France and is accordingly buried in the National Cemetery in Chattanooga. He died in 1988 at the age of ninety-four.

In March 2003, the Chattanooga Regional History Museum opened an exhibit in the metropolitan airport at Lovell Field to honor Harry Porter and to display some of the memorabilia that he had acquired during his lengthy aviation career. Originally located in the Baggage Claim area of the airport as a tribute to Porter, it has since been donated to the Chattanooga Regional History Museum whose future is in transition. On June 12, 2017, the successor to the Regional History Museum, the Chattanooga History Museum, transferred legal title and all literary property rights of Porter to the Chattanooga Public Library and University of Tennessee at Chattanooga.

Hopefully the community will recognize the importance of preserving this important part of aviation history and the memories of the contributions of Harry Porter.

Joe Engel – Barnum of Baseball

Organized baseball has had several characters in its long history since Abner Doubleday founded the game, but probably the two zaniest characters were Bill Veeck of the Chattanooga White Sox and Joe Engel of the Chattanooga Lookouts.

With the developers pushing for a new baseball stadium on the Southside near the river, Chattanooga may have three homes for one of the oldest baseball franchises in the country – before the wrecking ball destroys two present ballparks.

It is too late to help Kirkman Vocational High School as it fell with the construction of AT&T Stadium on Hawk Hill. Historic Engel Stadium appears to be the most likely target for the ever-expanding alleged needs of Erlanger Medical Center. With the need for more medical facilities with the COVID-19 pandemic, the hallowed ground on 3rd Street may also become an icon of the past.

We can only speculate about what the "Barnum of the Bushes" would have to say about the present threat to his beloved temple of entertainment. Joe Engel was born on March 12, 1893, in Washington, D.C. As a right-handed pitcher, he spent nine seasons in baseball with 1913 and 1914 with the Washington Senators where he acquired a record of seventeen wins against twenty-three losses before a sore arm. His career was over at the age of twenty-seven.

Much has been written about Engel's career as a scout and the development of his relationship with Clark Griffin, the Senators' manager and subsequent owner of the club. Engel became close friends with legendary pitcher Walter "Big Train" Johnson, and they bonded over a mutual love of fox hounds.

Griffith eventually appointed Engel as the club's first full-time scout, and he successfully served in that capacity for ten years. He was credited with signing most of the talent that led to Washington's winning pennants in 1924, 1925 and 1933, and including future Hall of Fame inductee, Joe Cronin.

Engel also had a vaudeville act in the off season with the two Senators' pitchers, Al Schardt and Nick Altrock . Their baseball comedy act lasted much longer than their playing careers. In 1929 Engel and Clark

Griffith schemed to buy the Chattanooga franchise in the Class A Southern League. Griffith has previously attempted to buy the Atlanta Crackers but was turned down. As a result, Engel acted as a straw man and buyer of record of the Chattanooga team.

Chattanooga welcomed Engel and his team with open arms. He first re-named the team Lookouts and spent $180,000 to build the present stadium to seat about 10,000 fans. With Engel's zany tactics, more than 17,000 fans exceeded the grandstand capacity on Opening Day in 1930. His use of promotional events was endless, and the limited space in this article does not adequately describe his efforts which are legendary and justify further review by Googling his name and that of the Chattanooga Lookouts. A seven-page article by Warren Corbell under "Joe Engel/Society for American Baseball Research" is particularly informative.

Among the stunts put on was his re-signing of seventeen-year-old left-handed female pitcher, Jackie Mitchell, who struck out both Lou Gehrig and Babe Ruth in 1931 after Engel signed her to a minor league contract. It was declared invalid the next day by baseball Commissioner Kennesaw Mountain Landis. Mitchell claimed her pitching to the Sultan of Swat and the Iron Horse was legitimate, but Engel would later admit that it was a "hoax" and that Ruth and Gehrig agreed to go along with the stunt. Also, in 1931 Engel traded a shortstop to Charlotte for a twenty-five-pound turkey which he cooked and fed to sportswriters. When asked about the sale, Engel quipped, "The turkey was having a better season."

Opening Day every year brought some type of fascinating extravaganza. Every April schools closed for students to attend. One year Engel re-enacted Custer's Last Stand, but this time Custer won the battle. On May Day in 1936, Engel put on his most successful stunt giving away a house, which also included a car in the garage, before 24,639 fans. Because of concern over the safety of the fans who were crowded on the sideline, Engel froze the baseballs to make sure they were too heavy to knock one into the crowd.

"Cash & Carry" was a popular annual event. An armored car dumped piles of mostly nickels on the field. A selected fan got to keep all he could scoop up in a designated period of time. Later Clark Griffith appointed his nephew, Calvin Griffith, as the new president of the

Lookouts, and he did not believe in Engel's outrageous promotions. As a result, attention dropped considerably. Engel prevailed on Clark to sell him the Lookouts if he could raise the money by selling $5.00 shares.

With Engel's popularity with the fans, 1,200 bought stock worth $30,000 in two months. Engel put in $47,000 of his own money, and Griffith rewarded him with a $25,000 bonus to support the local ownership of the Lookouts. As a result of the campaign to raise money for stock purchases, Engel planned to put on the biggest promotion on Opening Day in the history of the franchise. Engel intended to conduct an elephant hunt which aroused the opposition of the local Humane Society. With the advent of television, minor league attendance dropped. Chattanooga didn't escape the decline. The last big year with strong attendance was the pennant winning team of 1952, with 252,000 fans attending the games.

Refusing to integrate the Southern League by using black players, the league folded in 1961. With Engel Stadium sitting empty in 1962, the club formed an alliance with the Philadelphia Phillies as a member of the Double A South Atlantic League.

Joe Engel contributed much to the Chattanooga community. During the 1929 depression, he fed 11,000 fans for free and used the stadium as a soup kitchen and warehouse. At Christmas, he purchased 7,500 board games featuring his former teammate and friend, Walter Johnson, in order that needy children would have a Merry Christmas.

One of his most popular creations was the Joe Engel's Knothole Gang which had their own special section of seats inside the ballpark. The only requirements for free admission to the Lookouts games were good grades and regular attendance at church and school.

Organized baseball left Chattanooga in 1966. Joe Engel died in 1969, "Still striving daily to keep the eyes of the national baseball world focused on Chattanooga." Whether his cause of death was medical or a broken heart due to the demise of his beloved Lookouts remains unknown.

His memory deserves preservation of "the house that Joe Engel built." The efforts of the Engel Foundation in that direction deserve the community's support to avoid the wrecking ball demolishing another historical treasure.

Willie Six
Sewanee's African American Gentleman

The term "Sewanee Gentleman" has a connotation that differs with various groups in society. To the loyal supporters of the University of the South (Sewanee) it stands for a tradition of characteristics of high ethics, loyalty, and a benevolent attitude between the races. To detractors of the liberal arts university on the Cumberland Plateau, it invokes criticism for hanging on to outdated traditions carved by its pro-Southern founders before and after the Civil War.

Over the years since its inception in 1858, Sewanee has evolved from an all-male institution whose tradition has changed to allow the admission of women in 1969, in spite of strong objection by some member of the Board of Trustees. The first African American student was Nathaniel Owens from Hartselle, Tennessee. He enrolled in 1966 and graduated with honors. He was a star athlete in football and wrestling in 1970.

The school adhered to many of its paternalistic viewpoints pertaining to the issues of integration-segregation during the 1960's, but some faculty members and students regularly attended the controversial Highlander Folk School in Monteagle. In the Civil Rights era, it was a teaching institution which included Dr. Martin Luther King as one of its attendees. In 1969, a group of Sewanee professors were plaintiffs in a lawsuit that successfully advocated integration of the races in the Franklin County school system that included the Sewanee Elementary School.

One of the most loved and respected minority people at Sewanee was Willie Sims (Willie Six). Willie Sims was born in Pelham, Tennessee, on an unknown date near 1886, establishing his age at death between 62 and 69. He allegedly moved to Sewanee around 1901, and in 1907 he began working on a crew that built the loved All Saints Chapel.

For four years, he would work construction at the chapel in the morning, and in 1908 Sewanee's football coach arranged for him to become the trainer for the university's athletic teams, where he served until he retired in 1947.

During this era Sewanee was a member of the Southeastern Conference and regularly beat present day members Tennessee, Auburn,

Alabama, Georgia Tech, Texas, LSU, Texas A&M and Ole Miss on the gridiron. Only the Vanderbilt Commodores were able to avoid defeats by the Sewanee Tigers in a bitter rivalry.

"Willie Six" received his nickname because he wore a purple sweater with that number on the front. During the period he served, he traveled with the athletic teams throughout the South during the segregation era. It remains a mystery to this day as to where he would stay on the trips in centers of segregation such as Birmingham, New Orleans and Nashville, although he would be present on the sidelines when the games began after he had performed his usual duties as trainer for the team.

One of the legends surrounding Willie Six was that he never saw an opposing team score a touchdown. When they approached the Sewanee goal line, he would turn away.

When he retired in 1947 after 39 years as trainer, he was honored at the last home football game of that season by having it designated "Willie Six Day." He was carried off the field by the student athletes and given a pension that former athletes and students raised on his behalf.

A public thoroughfare, Willie Six Road, is named in his honor, and when he died in January 1950 his funeral was held in All Saints Chapel, signifying the first African-American to be given that honor. Members of Sewanee athletic teams served as pallbearers, and he is buried in the University Cemetery along with former officers in the Confederate Army. His grave is marked by a tombstone that was designed and donated by white former players.

One of the numerous testimonies about Willie Six was printed in the campus newspaper after his funeral, "He was universally considered the prototype of the Sewanee Gentleman."

Race relations have significantly changed over the years, but sixty-eight years after his death in 1950, the legend of Willis Six lives on at the University of the South. In a presentation by Vice-Chancellor John McCardell, Jr. on August 29, 2017, he spoke on Sewanee's relationship to the Confederacy in light of the controversies surrounding monuments of Rebel officers and heroes throughout the South.

He concluded his remarks by quoting one of Willie Six's favorite sayings, "The best year is the one comin' up."

He was "Sewanee's African American Gentleman."

Lon S. Varnell
Sewanee's Coaching Showman (1913-1991)

In a 1969 article in "Sports Illustrated," Lon Shelton Varnell was described as being a, "Coach, Methodist Minister, coal mine operator, car dealer, political campaign manager, hardware store proprietor and promoter of high-class entertainment in forty-nine states and Canada." As a sign that Lon Varnell was destined to be a big person in life, his birth weight was thirteen pounds, which was recognized in Ripley's Believe It or Not as a record.

Lon Varnell

Born in Adamsville, Tennessee, Varnell was a three-sport letterman in high school and college at Freed-Hardeman College and Bethel College in West Tennessee before entering the coaching field. He first coached basketball at Bethel, Southern Methodist University, and the University of Kentucky under the famed Adolph Rupp before he migrated to the University of the South (Sewanee) in 1948 to be head coach. Varnell also officiated as a referee in basketball games. He worked a Kentucky versus Fort Knox game in 1943 and a Kentucky versus Vanderbilt game in 1946, which allowed him to get to know Coach Rupp. That blossomed into a personal relationship.

Although he learned the use of a tight man-to-man defense from Rupp, during his twenty-two years of heading the Sewanee Tigers, he primarily employed a zone defense. Even being ordained as a Methodist minister, Varnell would sometimes display the use of some salty and explicit language against referees that he thought were mistreating his players. Sewanee, being a non-athletic scholarship school, required Varnell to recruit players with excellent academic records who could qualify for financial aid, or young men from prominent families that could pay for their sons to attend Sewanee.

During his tenure at Sewanee, his teams established a commendable record against teams with athletic scholarship players. Playing against taller and more talented squads, the Tigers defeated Georgia Tech, Florida State, Ole Miss, Mississippi State and others.

In 1951 he took his team to Europe and North Africa during the summer tour and won fifty-three of fifty-seven games played. This tour was a first in American intercollegiate sports and concluded with Sewanee winning the World Tournament in Geneva, Switzerland. The Sewanee team toured with the Harlem Globetrotters on part of the trip.

He developed a relationship with Abe Saperstein, founder and coach of the Harlem Globetrotters, which resulted in the squad in 1949 being the first all-black squad to play in the South at an engagement in Chattanooga. The Globetrotters game continues on a yearly basis today.

Varnell would later form the Harlem Magicians in 1953 using former Globetrotter stars such as the famed dribbler, Marquis Haynes, and the popular Goose Tatum among others. His 1955 Magicians would play in front of the first integrated audience in Atlanta. The competition with the Globetrotters led to Varnell's friend Saperstein filing a lawsuit in federal court in New York in late 1961 against Lon Varnell for alleged violation of Harlem Globetrotters' registered trademarks "Harlem Globetrotters," and "Magicians of Basketball" by promoting Harlem Magicians. In 1964, the lawsuit was settled with a consent decree agreed to by the former business associates.

During his coaching career, Varnell compiled a record of 215 wins against 98 losses, with one Collegiate Athletic Conference (CAC) championship in 1966. He remains Sewanee's all-time leader in basketball wins (215) as a head coach and was inducted into the Tennessee Sports Hall of Fame in 1973.

In the field of baseball, he set up a fall tour in the mid 1950's with two teams of black major leaguers who barnstormed throughout the South. These included Willie Mays, Hank Aaron, Don Newcombe, Joe Black, Ernie Banks, Roy Campanella, etc.

After retiring from coaching in 1970, he started Varnell Enterprises and established himself as a leading promoter in entertainment events that included stars such as Bill Cosby, Rolling Stones, Willie Nelson, Waylon Jennings, Elton John, Sonny & Cher, the Oak Ridge Boys, Elvis Presley, Lawrence Welk and Liberace.

His record at Sewanee is perpetuated each year with the Lon Varnell Classic that opens the season for the Tigers. When he died of cancer in 1991 at the age of seventy-seven, he was survived by his wife Kathryn, three sons and a daughter.

The Majors
Tennessee Football Family

Little did he know, while he was cutting hair as a barber or farming in Lynchburg, that he, Shirley Majors (1913-1981,) would become the patriarch of Tennessee's most famous football family.

He started the football program in nearby Huntland, and after his first-year record of 3-5, won 70 of his team's next 71 games. Utilizing the talents of his 159-pound tailback son, Johnny, in its single wing offense at Huntland, Coach Majors matriculated to the University of the South where he coached for twenty-one years, compiling a record of 93-74-5 in a Division 3 non-scholarship program.

His lifelong companion was his diminutive wife, Elizabeth, who was a school teacher and a "mother" to many Sewanee students and athletes. She was described by her daughter as, "Full of energy like a piece of dynamite." Many a Sewanee athlete and student enjoyed the warm hospitality she and her husband provided at their home. Their union produced five sons, Johnny, Joe, Bill, Larry and Bobby, and a daughter, Shirley Anne.

During his tenure at Sewanee, Coach Majors had two undefeated teams (1958 and 1963) and mentored six small college All-Americans and won five College Athletic Conference (CAC) championships.

Johnny graduated from Huntland, and while at Tennessee, was the 1956 SEC Most Valuable Player. He became an All-American and runner up to the Heisman Trophy winner, Paul Horning, of Notre Dame. Retired Chattanooga lawyer Hugh Garner was on the squad.

A coach like his father, Johnny Majors would win a national championship at Pittsburg in 1976 with Heisman Trophy winner Tony Dorsett. John would return to his alma mater in Knoxville in 1977, and during his 15 years as head coach of the Volunteers, he posted 115 SEC victories which placed him among the top ten SEC coaches in victories. During his coaching career at U.T., he won three SEC championships, and his teams were a perennial post season bowl participant.

Brother, Joe Majors, would play at Florida State and had a brief career with the Houston Oilers in the National Football League. He graduated from law school and would serve as a lobbyist in the Tennessee General Assembly.

Bill Majors was also an outstanding defensive player for the Vols and tried out with the Buffalo Bills. He would be an assistant coach at Tennessee. He was killed in a car-train collision on October 18, 1965, at the age of 26, with two other assistant coaches, Charlie Rash and Bob Jones.

Larry Majors played wingback for his father at Sewanee and graduated in 1963. He has coached and been an active member of the community since his graduation. He was elected to the Sewanee Sports Hall of Fame in 2019, based on his athletic ability and civic activities.

Shirley Majors

The youngest male member of the Majors clan is Bobby Majors, an All-American defensive player for the Vols in 1971. Bob played in the National Football League and is a businessman in Chattanooga.

Shirley Anne Majors kept up the family tradition of being an outstanding high school basketball player and a cheerleader at U.T. There she met her brother Bill's roommate and Vols player, Tom Husband, who would be her future husband.

In 1966 the Majors parents and athletes were inducted into the Tennessee Sports Hall of Fame as a family.

Coach Shirley Major and his wife, Elizabeth, the "First Lady of Tennessee Football" could be very proud of all six of their offspring. (and they were!)

John Wilkes Booth at Sewanee

The history of the University of the South, Sewanee, and the surrounding area is filled with many stories of unusual happenings and events. The presence of Al Capone in Monteagle, John Dillinger at Beersheba Springs, and the many ghosts of Sewanee are just part of the intrigue that surrounds the institute of higher learning established in 1858 on the Cumberland Plateau between Chattanooga and Nashville.

Another fascinating story in local folklore is the question of whether John Wilkes Booth, assassin of President Abraham Lincoln, actually died in a barn fire on April 26, 1865, near Port Royal, Virginia, while being pursued by federal troops.

The killing of President Lincoln by Booth has been well documented, and the theory of the assailant not being the body in the burning barn has not been strongly believed by many, but the theory is still advocated by a few naysayers.

In 1997, author Patricia Short Makris in her book *The Other Side of Sewanee*, included a paragraph about a Booth rumor that he was seen in the Sewanee Depot Village, "During the latter part of 1871 and early 1872." Another story asserted that he had pawned his watch at a local store. It was later claimed and allegedly verified that he had married a Sewanee woman (Louisa Price Payne) and had fathered a daughter by her.

Makris in a paragraph on Booth raises the questions of whether the man allegedly seen at Sewanee had gotten away with murdering Abraham Lincoln or had been one of the greatest impostors that ever lived.

Former *Chattanooga Free-Press* reporter, John Wilson, interviewed University of the South historiographer Arthur Ben Chitty in June 1992, and he claimed that he believed that Booth was in Sewanee and married a local girl in 1872.

Chitty and another colleague, Nathaniel Orlowek, a thirty-four year old religious educator at Beth Shalom Congregation in Potomac, Maryland, believed enough in their 1872 Sewanee theory that they wanted to exhume Booth's body from the Green Mount Cemetery in Baltimore, Maryland. He had originally been buried in great secrecy on April 28, 1865, under the floor of the Arsenal at the Washington Navy

Yard prior to being removed to the Booth family plot at Green Mount Cemetery in 1869.

Dr. Chitty questioned the identification of the body by Booth's older brother, Edwin Booth, when it was exhumed in 1869 as being, "Carefully staged."

Questions as to the identity of the individual that died in the barn arose intermittently and formed much of the basis for Chitty's and others' contentions that John Wilkes Booth did not die in the fire but escaped and was in Sewanee in 1872.

Documentary evidence at the Franklin County Courthouse in Winchester show a marriage record dated February 24, 1972, of John W. Booth to Louisa P. Payne, as well as a tax record for John W. Booth saying that he resided in the 18th District in Sewanee. Micayah, step-son from Louisa's first marriage, always maintained that John Wilkes Booth was his step-father.

Another rumor existed that, while in Sewanee, "Booth performed for the students at the University exhibitions of sleight-of-hand and readings from plays on Saturday night."

In 1994, Chitty, Orlowek and twenty-two descendants of Booth filed a court petition seeking to exhume the body at Green Mount and to have it examined to determine the age, sex, race and evidence of Booth's broken leg when he jumped from the stage at Ford's Theatre after shooting President Abraham Lincoln. The petition was denied, and an appeal was also unsuccessful in 1996. The opinion by a three-judge panel held that there was overwhelming evidence that indicated that Booth did died in the barn fire in 1865, and that his body was transferred to Green Mount in 1869.

An individual named Daniel E. George committed suicide in Enid, Oklahoma, in 1903. Prior to his death he claimed he was John Wilkes Booth. He allegedly had earlier confessed the same to a lawyer, Finis L. Bates. Bates claimed that he had acquired possession of the mummified body of Booth. He wrote a book in 1907, *Escape and Suicide of John Wilkes Booth*, which claimed that Booth had changed his name to John St. Helen until he committed suicide in 1903.

After the successful publication of his book, Bates displayed the mummified body he claimed was Booth at carnivals and side shows throughout the country for an admission fee. It was photographed at Jay Gould's "Million Dollar Spectacle." The mummy was subsequently kidnapped and is now missing.

In 1977 the book and movie adaptation, *The Lincoln Conspiracy*, revived public interest in the conspiracy theory. With the improvement and advancement in the accuracy of DNA scientific testing, Booth descendants may once again attempt to exhume his body to solve the long-standing question of whether John Wilkes Booth is buried in Baltimore, Maryland.

Anyone interested in the Chitty-Orlowek theory pertaining to the death of John Wilkes Booth or the alleged impostor should start with reading John Wilson's lengthy aforementioned article at The Public Library in Chattanooga. A trip to the library at the University of the South in Sewanee can further your curiosity by reviewing Arthur Ben Chitty's extensive collection of books on Booth that are present in the archives.

Did John Wilkes Booth survive the barn fire and reside at Sewanee? This is a perplexing question for history and conspiracy theorists.

John Wilkes Booth

Sewanee's Dr. William C. Gorgas & The Panama Canal

One of the most distinguished graduates of the University of the South (Sewanee) would have to be Dr. William Gorgas, October 3, 1854 - July 3, 1920.

Gorgas was born in Toulminville, Alabama, and his family moved to Sewanee in 1869 when he was 14 years of age. His father, Josiah Gorgas, was a Confederate General who initially became superintendent of what would eventually become Sewanee Military Academy, and who later would be the second vice-chancellor of the college.

After graduating from Sewanee, William attended Bellevue Hospital Medical College in New York City. He would be appointed to the United States Medical Corps in 1880, attaining the rank of Surgeon General of the Army.

While a student at Sewanee, he and three other students volunteered to go to New Orleans, Louisiana, to assist in the fight against a yellow fever epidemic that killed over 500 persons including two of Gorgas' fellow students. Although he was not the originator of the medical theory that the diseases of yellow fever and malaria were caused by transmission of the viruses by the bite of mosquitoes, Gorgas capitalized on the previous work of Army doctor, Major Walter Reed, and Cuban physician, Carlos Finlay.

Gorgas originally gained recognition for his work in controlling yellow fever and malaria in the State of Florida. This was followed by successful control and elimination of the diseases in Havana, Cuba, after the end of the Spanish-American War in 1898.

Using Reed and Finlay's prior works that demonstrated that mosquitoes of a certain type transmitted yellow fever into human populations, he was able to lead a movement that eradicated yellow fever and malaria in Cuba.

Gorgas' methods of either draining or covering all sources of standing water with kerosene to prevent mosquitoes from laying eggs and larvae from developing were highly successful. He further adopted the practice of isolating disease stricken patients with screening and netting.

Gorgas' successes did not come without controversy. Government health officials in America believed that yellow fever was caused by environmental filth and not from the bites of mosquitoes, and they vigorously attempted to discredit his work.

France had previously abandoned its efforts to build the Panama Canal on the Isthmus of Panama as the result of the death of 23,000 workers to yellow fever transmitted by mosquitoes. Gorgas, upon learning of the United States government's decision to build the Panama Canal, requested assignment to Panama. He initiated a broader program of sanitation controls against mosquitoes than those used in Cuba.

By 1906, he had eradicated yellow fever and was able to bring malaria under containment during the ten year period of successful construction and completion of the Panama Canal in 1914.

Gorgas was elected president of the American Medical Association in 1908 and in 1914 was appointed by President Woodrow Wilson to be Surgeon General of the Army.

On the basis of high costs, he still received opposition from his superiors to the public health measures that he advocated for adoption during the First World War. After the end of WWI, Gorgas continued to be a strong advocate for the effective control of infectious diseases with foreign governments. He received numerous honors and awards for his efforts.

While in London, England, on a stopover on a trip to Africa in 1920, he suffered a major stroke. While on his deathbed he was knighted by King George V and upon his demise lay in state in St. Paul's Cathedral prior to being returned to America for burial at Arlington National Cemetery in Washington, D.C.

Col. William C. Gorgas, hospital grounds, Ancon, Panama. Photo courtesy E. Hallen

PLACES

Burritt College
"Pioneer of the Cumberlands"

On the southern and northern extremities of the Cumberland Plateau are two institutions of higher learning in the nineteenth century (1848 and 1858) that have taken different historical destinations.

The University of the South at Sewanee was established by the Episcopal Church with the financial support of the multiple dioceses. This support has allowed it to survive and often to be described as the "Harvard of the South."

Burritt College, above Spencer in Van Buren County, was created by the Church of Christ denomination which had broken off from the larger Presbyterian Church over a split of involvement in the Mexican War in 1898 and several other issues. As a result, the college was never able to obtain the strong financial support that Sewanee received and that allowed it to survive as an educational institution. Burritt struggled from lack of resources from its creation in 1848 until it closed its doors in 1938.

The story of Burritt College is also the story of Van Buren County. The town of Spencer was created purely by parents who enrolled their children in the college and then moved to the rural village to reduce many of the costs of education. It was the desire of the citizens of Spencer to establish an institution of learning superior to that of the local schools that led to the creation of Burritt College.

In addition, the lack of good transportation and the isolation of the community contributed to the citizens being in favor of the new school. Isolated by rough roads from the nearest towns of McMinnville (eighteen miles west) and Sparta (fifteen miles north), it was extremely difficult to travel to and from because of the mountainous terrain.

The school provided elementary, high school and college training and was the main source of education in the mountainous region of Van Buren County.

The school first opened on February 26, 1848 with seventy-three students and three teachers under the leadership of President Isaac Newton Jones. He was a native of McMinn County and had been one of the main original supporters of the idea of the creation of Burritt.

Although not a possessor of academic training needed to be the head of the school, Jones did establish the type of curriculum which Burritt would follow without change for sixty years during its existence. The basic courses were classical in nature and included languages, philosophy, mathematics and Christianity.

Jones was succeeded by William Davis Carnes in 1830, and he introduced co-educational classes at Burritt in spite of some opposition of supporters of the school and citizens of Spencer. In spite of Jones prevailing on the mixing of the sexes, he was forced to establish stringent rules which included the prohibition of all oral and written communications between the students, except with permission of the faculty and at athletic events and heavily chaperoned events.

In spite of its restrictions, the issue of co-education established Burritt as the Pioneer in the South of joint education.

Chapel attendance was made a part of the curriculum, and daily attendance at religious exercises was required of all students, as well as the practice of Bible reading.

Despite the efforts of Carnes to lay the foundation to instill the students with ethics of "virtues, honesty and perseverance" necessary to set a high moral and religious tone, a number of problems with discipline developed.

The main problem that arose was the access of "moonshine whiskey" in the area, including the proprietorship of a preacher "of great influence" in the community. Violations of the "no liquor" rule led to the expulsion of several students, many from prominent families.

During the Civil War, the school closed in 1861 as the result of many students enrolling in the Confederate Army.

Throughout the years of its existence, Burritt College provide a cathedral of learning with a strict moral code that was tightly controlled but provided a quality education. The size of the student body ebbed and rose during its years of existence. Burritt's basic financial problem was its lack of any endowment. Without significant voluntary contributions, the school became more dependent upon the Van Buren County Board of Education for financial support as the school became the source of public education in the county on the high school level.

The advent of the public education system started the end of Burritt College in 1936. With the establishment of a county operated high school, Burritt's existence was short-lived, and the last years of the school's existence was 1937-1938. Only two buildings remained in existence.

A comprehensive ninety-six-page paper written on the history of Burritt College by Marian West around 1968-1970 titled "Pioneer of the Cumberland, A History of Burritt College 1848-1939" is informative. The paper was written by West while he was a student at Tennessee Technological University in Cookeville. It provides an excellent historical summary of the reason for the creation of the school, its philosophy of teaching students moral conduct, curriculum emphasizing religious and classical history, and the story of the school's course of existence until it closed in 1939.

In 2013, the Burritt College Museum in Spencer, Tennessee, was established. The first curator, Bonnie Adcock, has been extremely helpful in providing visitors with valuable information involving the history of Burritt.

Burritt was described in one of its promotional brochures distributed to families of prospective students and church groups as an institution with, "A beautiful campus, Christian influence, splendid gymnasium and electric lights."

Unfortunately, the lack of foresight to establish a sound endowment program resulted in the final demise of an institution providing a quality education to its students.

Burrett College in Spencer, Tennessee

Beersheba Springs Mountain Resort

In 1833 Beersheba Porter Cain discovered a chalybeate (mineral spring waters containing iron salts) spring in the mountainous region of Grundy County outside of Altamont, Tennessee.

The little village that was above Collins River Valley would become incorporated in 1839 and would function as a summer hotel and included log cabins to escape the summer heat below and to avoid various diseases.

The purchase of the property in 1854 by Louisiana slave trader, Colonel John Armfield, led to a period of development that included a luxurious hotel that would accommodate four hundred guests. Armfield brought upwards of one hundred slaves to upgrade the property and build the buildings.

The resort added ice houses, billiard rooms, and bowling alleys. Armfield also planted many shade and fruit trees during this period and imported musicians from New Orleans to perform at the dances held on the premises. French chefs were also imported from Louisiana to provide fine cuisines for the guests.

Armfield also tried to induce two Bishops in the Episcopal Church to consider the area as a possible location for the University of the South to educate Episcopal youth.

Two homes were built for Bishops James Otey and Leonidas Polk of Louisiana who would be instrumental in the selection of the site for the new university. Unfortunately the Sewanee Mining Company offered ten thousand free acres of land outside of Monteagle which was accepted in 1857 and the location was confirmed at a meeting of the Sewanee Board of Trustees in Beersheba.

During the Civil War the property was sold to Northern investors. From the wooden observatory at the front of the hotel skirmishes between Confederate and Union troops in the valley below could be observed.

During the Civil War, the residents were constantly harassed by federal forces and bushwhackers (homeless ex-soldiers) who plundered, pillaged, and robbed whenever they could. Surprisingly, all of the property remained intact in spite of raids by the federals and outlaws.

On September 20, 1871, Armfield died, and the resort went through many up and down periods. The isolation of the location and substandard roads was always a problem, but the resort still remained an attractive destination because of its beauty.

Various routes have been built to make the area more accessible. Roads to Chattanooga, Gruetli, and McMinnville were connected during the post-Civil War period. The Dixie Highway (U.S.41) constructed during the 1920's from Chicago to Florida was one of the first steps to provide accessibility to the area.

In 1926 Tennessee Highway 56 was built up the mountain to Beersheba. Unfortunately the blasting put an end to the mineral springs which originally created the resort. The Great Depression and the loss of the springs negatively affected the property, and it was bought and sold several times.

Although better roads to the resort were now available, the post-Depression recovery in 1939-1941 did not revive Beersheba Springs. However, several famous visitors have stayed at the resort over the years. Prior to his presidency, Franklin Pierce, the fourteenth president of the United States stayed at Beersheba Springs. In 1840 Tennessee Governor and future president, James Polk, held a political rally at the location.

In 1934 an individual who identified himself as Boshee Bouch was a short time resident. In reality he was Public Enemy No. 1, John Dillinger. He got along with the residents who helped him dig a well on his property which contained a simple cabin. Others sold him vegetables while he was at Beersheba Springs prior to being shot and killed by the FBI in July of 1934 in Chicago.

After years of neglect, the property and facilities were bought for $3,000 by the Tennessee Conference of the Methodist Church to be used as retreat grounds in November 1941. The Methodists have maintained ownership since that time and have continuously upgraded and improved the premises. Over the years, all of the modern convenience of electricity, water, telephone, and even wireless access has been added as well as complete modernization of the buildings and cabins.

In 1955 Beersheba Springs was incorporated as a town with 4.9 square miles of territory and a city manager-council form of government.

Since 1967 the community has hosted the Beersheba Springs Arts and Craft Festival each year on the fourth weekend in August. It usually has over 200 vendors and is attended by thousands of visitors.

In 1980 the historic district of the town was placed on the National Register of Historic Places.

The history of this quaint and beautiful place has been preserved by the combining of three articles by Herschel Gower, Carl Elkins, and Ann Hale Trout covering the earliest days of its existence through 2010.

Googling Beersheba Springs on your computer will provide the reader with a wealth of data and inspire them to take a scenic trip to this historical part of Grundy County.

Beersheeba Springs in its heyday - from the Cline Collection

Chattanooga's Law School

With the proliferation of new law schools in Knoxville and Nashville, Chattanooga is the only large Tennessee community that does not have a law school. Such was not the case from 1898 through 1960.

The Chattanooga Law School was begun as the Law Department of Grant University, predecessor to the University of Chattanooga, and was housed in a building that capped the Hill overlooking the University between Oak Street and McCallie Avenue. It was later torn down to be replaced by the brick buildings of the University.

Robert Pritchard, author of the "Treatise on Wills and Administration of Estates," which was the legal authority on said subjects, was the first Dean of the school.

After serving as Dean for twelve years, he was replaced by Judge Lewis Shepherd, considered by many to be one of the most skillful and talented lawyers in the history of the legal community.

The individual most closely identified with the development of the law school was Charles T. Evans, who served as Dean from 1901-1910 and increased the enrollment until it was the third largest law school in the South, ranking only behind Virginia and Texas Law Schools.

In 1910, the university's law school was dissolved, and Mr. Evans organized the Chattanooga College of Law and served as Dean until his death in 1920. The faculty consisted of practicing attorneys and elected judges. Judge W.B. Swaney became Dean upon the death of Mr. Evans and served in that capacity until 1946.

As a result of World War II draining the school of its students, the school closed.

In 1947 Roy McKenzie, Sr., president of McKenzie Business School, announced his intention to start a law school, either as a reactivation of the Chattanooga College of Law, or as a division of his business school. Although opposed by the Chattanooga Bar Association, the school opened with over one hundred students and some twenty part time instructors, who were practicing attorneys or judges.

The basis for the opposition by the bar association was an accusation that fourteen of the sixteen attorneys involved in the Chattanooga

Divorce Mill investigation had been graduates of the Chattanooga College of Law. In the scandal, it was found that spouses of soldiers were getting uncontested divorces without proper protection of the servicemen's rights under the federal Soldier and Sailors Relief Act when they were shipped out for military service in Europe or the Pacific

Roy McKenzie addressed the Chattanooga Bar Association and requested the association support his new school. The group of lawyers voted to cooperate with the school, although not approving it. Gus Wood, Jr. became the new Dean, and the practice of using part time professors from the legal and judicial communities continued.

Approximately half of the attorneys in Chattanooga during the first forty years of the 20th Century were graduates of the law school and at one time all the judges in the Chancery, Circuit and Criminal Courts were graduates.

With tightening standards on eligibility to take the bar examination and reduction in federal benefits for World War II Veterans, the student body registration declined.

However Korean War Veterans became eligible for educational benefits, and this allowed the school to remain open until 1960. In that year, the graduating class only had ten members.

Notable graduates for the Chattanooga College of Law included Alexander Guerry (1914), future headmaster of Baylor School and vice-chancellor of the University of Chattanooga and the University of the South. A talented trial lawyer, E.B. Baker (1928), and John Stophel (1955), member of one of Chattanooga's leading law firms, Chambliss Bahner and Stophel at the time of his death on October 4, 2007, were both excellent lawyers and/or community leaders.

One of the surviving graduates of the Chattanooga College of Law is Paul Leitner, Jr. (1954), who is the senior partner at Leitner, Williams, Dooley and Napolitan, one of the leading civil defense firms in the area.

The future will determine whether Chattanooga creates a need for another law school to compete with the other metropolitan areas.

American Temperance University Harriman, TN

Eighty miles northeast from Chattanooga towards Knoxville in Roane County lies a village known as Harriman. It was incorporated in 1890 as a community created out of the temperance movement against the manufacture and consumption of the "devil rum" (alcohol) which became active in the 1870's.

From the beginning, Harriman was to be a major center of the nationwide effort of the anti-alcohol group to permanently outlaw drinking alcohol in America. Harriman was known as the "Prohibition City of the Nation." The title to each deed registered at the courthouse contained a clause which stated that for every foot of real estate transferred a clause was written "prohibiting the making, using, handling, storing, or selling of intoxicating liquors" under the penalty of revoking the real estate transfer.

Harriman had originally been founded as the headquarters of the East Tennessee Land Company which built a modern three story office building that would initially be known as Temperance Hall after the movement. Unfortunately the land company failed, and the building became part of American Temperance University that was created in 1893.

Unique in the legislation that created Harriman were also certain restrictive laws which banned alcoholic beverages throughout the township, and the town's official city seal bore the motto, "Prohibition, Peace, and Prosperity."

In a 53 page Register of the American Temperance University for the 1897-1898 school year, the attributes of the University as well as Harriman and the surrounding countryside are described in promising detail to promote the community and school favorably.

Attracting non-drinking students from throughout the country that could easily be reached by several railroad systems, the school opened with its first class on September 12, 1893, with an enrollment of 250 students from 15 states. In 1887 the school reached its highest enrollment of 376 students and 20 states being represented.

In the Law Department, the Honorable H.B. Case of Chattanooga was listed as one of the lecturers. Although no Chattanoogan was identified as being enrolled at American Temperance University, Frank Richy of Cleveland was listed in the preparatory school as a student. Key City Book Store in Harriman was a branch office of T.H. Payne and Co. of Chattanooga as authorized agent for Roane County text books and school supplies.

Harriman was a city of 4,000 God-fearing citizens who enthusiastically welcomed the university. An auditorium was erected and initially named Greenleaf Hall in honor of the donor who contributed $30,000 to pay the cost necessary to build an attractive auditorium with a seating capacity of 1,200 students. After the school closed in 1908, the building was used as a jail. It has been preserved on the National Historic Registry and now houses the offices of the City of Harriman and has a historical museum in the basement.

Another three story brick building titled Munyon Hall served as a boarding house for the male students. There was no separate facility for female students, and it can only be assumed that they were housed in private residences.

The third building provided by the citizens of Harriman was a gymnasium which satisfied the mandatory requirement that all students take gymnasium exercise.

The school also had an active intramural and intercollegiate sports program. Over the years the school played many football games against the University of Tennessee and Maryville College in 1905-1906. The team lost to Maryville College seven times, and split ten games with the University of Tennessee with the most lopsided loss to the Volunteers being 104-0 in 1905. This score remains as the highest ever obtained by a UT team. In 1907 the squad defeated the University of Chattanooga by a score of 10-0.

The faculty at the schools zenith had over 20 instructors in six courses of study, a law school and a curriculum in post-graduate studies.

Unique for the school was affiliation with three other institutions in the state at Greeneville, Powell's Valley, and White Pine, where local students could take additional courses that could be used towards there degree at American Temperance University.

A four year course of study was also provided for those students studying to be teachers, and a preparatory school was created for freshman students deficient in the classic languages of Greek and Latin.

Foremost in the school's commitment to prohibition was a requirement that each student upon enrolling had to take the following pledge, "I hereby promise upon my honor to conform to all the laws and regulations of the American Temperance University, now enforced, or which may be enacted by the proper authorities, while I remain a student of the institution and to yield respectful obedience to all its constituted authorities."

Although the American Temperance University was only in existence from 1893-1908, it provided quality education to its students. Among its graduates were several notable individuals including two congressional members of the United States House of Representatives and a justice of the California Supreme Court.

The surviving buildings of the University have been taken over by the City of Harriman and private interests to preserve the historical significance of this important component of the temperance movement.

Americaan Temperance University

Camp Crossville World War II

Most Tennesseans do not know that there were prisoner of war camps in the Volunteer State during World War II. They were Camp Forrest near Tullahoma, Camp Campbell near Nashville, Camp Tyson in Henry County, and Camp Crossville in Cumberland County. They were part of 155 POW camps. Very little is left physically of any of these camps across the state except at Camp Crossville.

Ironically the same land that used to be the Crossville POW camp is now named for the grandson of one of America's greatest WWI military heroes, Alvin C. York, who was born and died in Fentress County adjacent to Cumberland County.

The Clyde York 4-H Center entertains thousands of children who go there every year to learn about archery, swimming, and teamwork as part of the teachings of the organization. The long white building near the entrance used to be part of a prisoner of war hospital.

A misconception amongst the public has been that Japanese POWs were kept in the camp, when in reality only German and a few Italian detainees were in Crossville. This was because it was known locally as "Jap Camp" on "Jap Camp Road." Camp Crossville housed over 1,500 German and Italian POWs between November 1942 and the camp's closing in December 1945.

A German officer, Gerhard G. Hennes, captured in North Africa in May 1943, became a POW at Camp Crossville and subsequently wrote a 128 page paperback book which described the two years that he was imprisoned in the camp. After World War II ended, Hennes would become an American citizen. In 2004, he published *The Barbed Wire: POW in the USA* which gives a detailed description of prison life at the facility. Unfortunately the book is listed on the internet for a price for a new book at $213.00 and $63.00 for a used copy.

From Hennes' description, things were pretty good for German prisoners in Crossville with good food, clothing, recreational facilities, paid jobs and even the right to travel freely in the Crossville area and leave the camp unescorted. Another account of POW life at Crossville was preserved in the memoir "Crossville: How Did We Treat Our POWs?"

One reason for the leniency of incarceration was the rural nature of the community. With so many local young men in the military, there was a shortage of manpower needed to work in factories and farms. The German POWs filled that deficiency.

Crossville has established the Military Memorial Museum at 20 South Main Street, Crossville, Tennessee, 38555 (931) 456-5520 which contains many artifacts and memorabilia about Camp Crossville as well as other military history items from the Civil War up to the present.

One interesting exhibit is a large wooden model of Camp Crossville that was created based on sketches and maps of the facility.

Robert Boring, curator of the museum, along with his wife, Nina, who is the director, supplied historical facts. "Camp Crossville is believed to be the oldest POW camp in the country. It specialized in the internment of German officers including 1,500 from Field Marshall Erwin Rommel's North Africa Corps. We also had 400 Italian officers at the camp, but they were transferred to other locations because of the friction between them and the Germans, as each side blamed the other for the defeat in the desert."

Other than the former hospital, the largest remaining structure at the camp is a massive brick chimney. Like most of the military facilities that were declared surplus property after the end of the War, most were sold at auctions and carried away by the bidders.

The prospect of a $3,000,000 economic benefit to the community by the construction of the camp relying heavily on local labor and resources strongly contributed to a more favorable outlook towards the POWs.

Although there were no successful escapes or espionage committed by the POWs, a frustrated FBI Director, J. Edgar Hoover, in the April 1944 issue of "American Magazine" warned the public how lax treatment of the POWs could lead to more escapes and listed several factors that should be watched to prevent such action. Unfortunately this provided the POWs considering a possible escape, "A complete blue print telling how to escape. Do it alone. Do not talk any more than absolute necessary. Go as far as quickly as you can. Have some cash."

Fortunately few attempted to escape which was probably because of the favorable conditions they were living under while POWs. A few examples of German arrogance remained, while their belief that Germany would still win the war remained. Some objected to learning English, as they thought that German would be the principal language spoken after the Nazis prevailed.

The lenient treatment came to a halt in 1945 after discovery of the atrocities committed against the Jews in the Holocaust. Although most POWs claimed ignorance of the crimes committed in the concentration camps, this did not stop the reduction in quality of food, paid labor, recreation privileges, and other benefits to which they had become accustomed.

A nineteen page article published in 2003 by Gregory Kupsky titled "To Win Our War With Butter and Beefsteaks – Camp Crossville and the Treatment of Axis Prisoners of War" is a well-written and comprehensive commentary on many issues involved in the handling of POWs brought to this country during WWII. It is worth obtaining by searching the internet.

A one-day trip to the Military Memorial Museum in Crossville will further educate the public about this relatively unknown piece of wartime history in Tennessee.

The Crosses at Sewanee

Motorists traveling east on Highway 41A from Cowan to Sewanee in Franklin County during the twilight or evening hours can witness a spectacular sight. As you start your upward ascent from the fertile farm land in the valley below, there looms an approximately sixty foot tall cross that is illuminated at night by electric lights. What is the history of this spectacular memorial cross?

Prior to the erection of this cross in 1922, a simple wooden cross twelve feet high had been constructed by Bishop Charles T. Quintard and others on March 22, 1868, at the community post office named University Place. In 1870 it would be re-named "Sewanee." This cross was located on what is now the current site of St. Lukes Hall on the campus of the university.

In the fall of 1921 a decision was made to erect a giant cross at the end of Tennessee Avenue overlooking the Franklin County valley on the edge of a bluff on the campus of the University of the South.

The purpose of the erection of the cross was to serve as a memorial to all who had died in World War I, "The War to End All Wars." It now honors not only those heroes from Franklin County who made the supreme sacrifice in the service of our country in World War I, but also a tribute to those who have been killed in each subsequent international conflict.

One morning a chapel talk by Dr. Ben Finney describing the community of interest existing between the University and the people of Franklin County resulted in the student body traveling to the proposed site to gather stones for the proposed Cross. An endowment for the electric bill to light the Cross was obtained by selling copies of the first edition of the *Sewanee Cook Book*.

At the base of the cross is a memorial plaque for each conflict which reads as follows:

World War I: *"To the sons of Sewanee who considered their country's call to service in the World War 1917-1918."*

World War II: *"To those from the university, the military academy, Sewanee, and all Franklin County in World War II 1941-1945."*

Korean War: *"To the students and citizens of Sewanee and to the citizens of Franklin County who served this country in the Korean War 1950-1953."*

Vietnam War: *"To the men and women of the University of Sewanee and of Franklin County who answered their call to serve in the Vietnam War 1965-1972."*

Desert Storm: *"To the men and women of the University of Sewanee, and of Franklin County who served in Desert Storm 1991."*

To reach the Cross one travels on a long, unpaved, country road towards the bluff overlooking the valley. As you approach the site of the memorial, it looms directly in front of your vehicle in the middle of the road that ends with a loop around the cross.

The site has served as a place to reflect on one's life, perform a wedding, pray for the lives of those memorialized, or just quietly enjoy the beautiful natural scenery. One visitor has described the site as, "Where God goes to think." Another has described it as a special place to them where they can go with the burdens of the world on their shoulders and they can leave with peace.

On March 22, 2016, another simple wooden cross was planted on the main campus on the occasion of the celebration of the sesquicentennial of Sewanee's second founding. The cross was created by the Physical Plant Services of the University from timbers originally used in 1860 and 1866 in the erection of the houses of the first Vice Chancellor, Bishop Leonidas Polk, and founder, George Fairbanks.

The cross was intended, "To be a lasting memento of the historical moment and has a permanent home in All Saints Chapel, the main place of worship on the campus."

A visit to the giant Cross also creates a lasting impression on those who make the pilgrimage to the site. During the spring when the foliage is blooming, and in the fall, changing of the colors add additional reflections as to the beauty and serenity of the Cross.

How Marr Field Became Lovell Field

The dedication of Detroit Buick Motor Company engineer, Walter L. Marr, to aviation has been well documented in the history of Chattanooga after he moved to the area and established a residence on Signal Mountain.

Marr was instrumental in establishing Chattanooga's first airport in East Chattanooga on the western side of Missionary Ridge. It was located between the railroad tracks and Dodson Avenue off Glass Street in East Chattanooga in 1919. Because of his commitment and support of aviation, the field with the primitive hangers was named Marr Field. He had not only been involved with the project through the Chamber of Commerce, he also worked with the Hamilton County Road Department to clear the area and set up a grass strip runway. He also operated one of the county tractors on the project.

Marr Field opened on November 23, 1919, with the first scheduled flights set to arrive on November 24 from Canton, Ohio. The facility was opened on Thanksgiving Day with stunt pilot, Eddie Stinson, providing paid rides to interested citizens in both the morning and afternoon. Because of bad weather, the dedication of the field had to be delayed until December 5.

Marr Field would always receive both positive and negative reviews.

Among the earliest arrivals on the day of dedication was Colonel W.L. Dargue, who was in charge of the United States Army air corps for the southeast. Dargue landed at Marr Field with John Lovell, chairman of the Chattanooga Chamber of Commerce as a passenger in his plane. Lovell was dedicated to the field of aviation and continued to improve and support Marr Field. His loyalty and dedication to the development of air service in Chattanooga would be rewarded later.

A dinner on the night of December 5 was held at the Chattanooga Golf and Country Club where Colonel Dargue was the guest speaker. In his address he praised Marr Field as being, "The leading facility in the South" and made predictions about the development of aviation.

Other pilots over the years were not quite so complimentary about the facility. Swirling crosswinds created by the location of Marr Field in the vicinity of Missionary Ridge on the eastern side of the five-hundred-foot-high natural barrier created severe problems for pilots attempting to land or take off or land, particularly in inclement weather and fog.

Although improvements had been made over the years, the field was still hindered by its location. Airline passenger service from Chicago, Illinois, to Atlanta, Georgia, with an intermediate stop in Chattanooga, had been established by the fledgling Interstate Airlines. Marr Field was the site of multiple crashes, and on March 20, 1927, one of the Interstate planes crashed in front of a viewing crowd.

Perhaps the death knell of the airfield occurred on December 28, 1928, when an airmail plane operated by Interstate Airlines crashed and killed the pilot and three passengers. After taking off on its route to Atlanta, the plane crashed and burned with motor trouble being alleged as the cause of the accident. A fifth occupant of the aircraft jumped just before the plane struck the ground and only sustained minor bumps and bruises. The plane crashed about a mile from Marr Field in the backyard of a residence at Ocoee Street and Orchard Knob Avenue. Those events would lead to numerous critical statements, demands for improved facilities, and crash investigations that would further lead to a search for a new location for the airport.

After the December 23rd crash, passenger service was suspended at Marr Field, and the erection of beacon lights designed for night flying were installed. Air mail service was allowed to continue but with additional conditions.

Despite the improvements, criticism continued and a scalding critique by L.T. Adhinion, an aviator and representative of the Texas Pacific Oil Company, claimed in an interview with a Chattanooga reporter in an article on January 18, 1929, that Marr Field was the "world's worst" because he could not land due to fog and had to be re-routed to another airfield west of the Brainerd Golf Course named Brainerd Field.

In not so glowing terms he said, "Marr Field is not an airport. It is more like a cow lot, and the hangers look like cowsheds. Neither of their airports, Marr Field or Brainerd are fit to land a $20,000 plane, and I am certainly sorry I stopped."

City leaders eventually purchased a farm along South Chickamauga Creek, and the new airport at its present location was established. It would be named Lovell Field in honor of John Lovell who had continuously worked on behalf of aviation in the Chattanooga area for many years. He would become the first manager of the field.

Marr Field would gradually fall into disuse and eventually closed. Little, if any, evidence remains today of what was Chattanooga's first developed airfield during the early days of aviation. Walter Marr would remain a resident of Signal Mountain and build a still existing showplace, Marrcrest, that still stands as a historical structure.

(Portions of this article were taken from a prior article by Harmon Jolley on July 20, 2009, on the Chattanoogan.com)

Marr Field as recorded in a scrapbook created by Ben King and salvaged by Arch Di Peppe.

Chamberlain Field
Turkey Day Football

From 1908 through 1973, college and high school football games were played on the University of Chattanooga (U.C.) campus at Chamberlain Field on Thanksgiving Day.

The field was originally named for university trustee and Civil War Union Captain, Hiram Chamberlain. It later also honored his son, Morrow Chamberlain, who was also a U.C. trustee.

Prior to 1908 when U.C. was Grant University, games were played at Orient Park.

The inaugural college football game was played in 1908 between the U.C. Moccasins and the 12th Calvary team from Fort Oglethorpe. U.C. prevailed by a score of 8-5.

The field featured a partially covered wooden grandstand. That structure was razed in 1927 to create a, "Beautiful concrete stadium with an exterior of brick and stone in harmony with the other buildings on the campus," at a cost of $50,000.

The stands on the Oak Street side contained a dormitory for the students and athletes on the second floor. The facility was dedicated in a game against Vanderbilt on September 24, 1927.

Over the years, high school rivalries were also fought on Chamberlain Field. City-Central and Baylor-McCallie games were amongst the most intense, but other teams such as Bradley County, South Pittsburg, Red Bank, Soddy Daisy, Rossville, and other schools played in Turkey Day games at Chamberlain.

The Vine Street (North) stands, which would be designated as the visitor's side, were also intended to run the entire length of the field, but because of unavailable funds, were shortened in length from only the fifty yard line to the goal line. As a result the stadium had an unbalanced appearance. This structure also included a dormitory. Prior to its razing, the Vine Street Commons Area was a meeting place over the years for students to socialize between classes.

The Oak Street stands were often filled with the University's biggest financial backers who often came to the games attired in business suits, ties, and furs to show their support for the Moccasins. (The reduced mascot name of Mocs came in later years after a protest by Tribal Cherokees and a vote of the student body.) The games were as much a social event as they were gridiron clashes. As a special benefit, a private room was set aside for a select group to partake of beverages which were not allowed in the stadium. The room was not available to the general public.

U.C. was an independent school and was not a member of any regular football conference until it joined the Southern Conference in 1976. As a result, several bigger schools would often play the local team on Thanksgiving Day with a sellout crowd of over 10,000 fans attending the games.

Many high school teams would play on the last Thursday in November. The heated City-Central rivalry would take place at Chamberlain beginning in 1917 in several Thanksgiving games during the sixty-year one rivalry.

The only tie game by U.C. on Thanksgiving took place in 1935 when the Moccasins and the Centre College Colonels fought evenly 7-7. In 1945 U.C. upset the Ole Miss Rebels 31-6 before a crowd of 7,500. In 1947 Booker T. Washington beat Howard in the first Turkey Day Classics between African American schools.

In 1970 the final Thanksgiving Day game at Chamberlain resulted in a 40-6 UTC victory over Jacksonville State (AL). A special feature of the game was an emotional pre-game speech to the Mocs team by former player, Phil Payne, who had been paralyzed in an off-the-field injury. A.C. "Scrappy Moore" ended a thirty-seven year coaching career in Chattanooga as the head football leader for the Moccasins on that date.

The final UTC game to be played on Chamberlain Field, although not on Turkey Day, was on October 4, 1997, with a victory against Wofford 20-17. At halftime the UTC band played "Auld Lang Syne" as a fitting tribute to the old structure that contained many memories for the university players, fans and community.

At the time UTC left Chamberlain Field for Finley Stadium on October 28, it was the second oldest NCAA Division I campus football stadium behind Harvard.

On April 18, 2008, a final event took place on the soon-to-be demolished stadium as the annual Blue-Gold spring inters-quad scrimmage was played, and the school asked former coach "Scrappy Moore" to serve as honorary coach.

When the Oak Street (South Stadium) was leveled, a final tribute to the old stadium was made by the University when it erected Chamberlin Pavilion which was constructed of the entrance sign and bricks from the original stadium.

The old stadium is gone but many memories remain.

Chamberlin Field

Chattanooga's Professional Football Team
Chattanooga Cherokees (1963-1966)

Local businessman Charles O. Ragan, Sr., had visions of making Chattanooga a hot bed of professional football when he created the Chattanooga Cherokees in 1962.

Ragan believed that the high interest in both high school and college teams in southeast Tennessee and northwest Georgia could be developed into professional football at one level below that of the National Football League (NFL).

The Cherokees played three seasons in the semi-professional Southern Football League in 1963-1965 and then merged with the North American Football League in 1966.

The team was comprised of many former high school and college players from the Chattanooga area, with University of Chattanooga players being a large component of the forty man roster.

The head coach for the Cherokees in 1963 was Ben Boulware who had been an assistant coach under Frank Fabris at Rossville High School when their 1962 team was undefeated and won the Georgia State Championship.

Notable among players in 1963 was Johnny Green, quarterback from the University of Chattanooga who had led the Moccasins to an upset victory over the University of Tennessee in 1958 and had been selected as a Little All American player. He also played four seasons in the American Football League with the Buffalo Bills and New York Titans from 1960-1963 prior to the merger of the NFL-AFL.

Cotton Letner from Ten Mile in Meigs County, Tennessee, was an outstanding player at the University of Tennessee in Knoxville. He was an end and placekicker for the Vols during the 1958-1960 season. His kicking was responsible for upset wins over Auburn (3-0) and LSU (14-13) in 1959. Letner played professional football with the Canadian Football League Montreal Alouettes and the Buffalo Bills in the AFL. He also would be a player/coach with the Cherokees.

Charles Benefield (Auburn), Joe Cash (Georgia), Mike Leinweber (Purdue), David Longley (Vanderbilt) and Emmett Wilson (Georgia

Tech) complimented the rest of the squad from smaller schools like U.C., Tennessee Tech, and Middle Tennessee.

During the first season of play in 1963, the Chattanooga team finished in third place in the Southern Football League with a record of 8-5-1.

During its seven home games played at the University of Chattanooga's Chamberlain Field, the team had fan attendance ranging from a low of 6,409 to a high of 12,076. Whether these numbers were a true reflection of paid attendance or the result of too many free tickets is unknown. The team originally had allowed all minors under the age of eighteen free admission to the Cherokee games. That was changed in 1964 to charge children over the age of twelve $2.00-$2.50, and to get the under-twelve discount they had to be accompanied by a paying adult.

Attendance at other stadiums in the eight member league was considerably lower and financial problems began to rise. In the championship game between the Daytona Beach Thunderbirds and the Jacksonville Robins on November 29, 1963, only 2,000 fans showed up in forty degree weather at the Gator Bowl for the title game.

One highlight of the season was when former City High defensive back, Jim East, ran a blocked field goal attempt back for a ninety-nine yard touchdown, a league record in that category.

The 1964 team was the most successful on the playing field with a record of nine wins and five losses but attendance continued to decline. Although the Cherokees played and lost (21-9) in the league championship game against the Daytona Beach Thunderbirds at Chamberlain Field, the announced attendance was only 1,000.

Former City High Coach and federal probation officer, Vic Varner, was the head coach with two assistants.

Former U.C. and American Football League player with the Buffalo Bills, Carey Henley, joined the squad as well as Tennessee Tech quarterback, Gordon Mason. Henley would later have a successful career as a high school football coach in the Chattanooga area at Kirkman, Brainerd, and Tyner prior to his death in 2013. Yet most of the team remained U.C. and local high school graduates. However, former U.T. Vol and Baltimore Colt standout, Bert Rechichar, did join the team as a place kicker.

By the 1965 season, fan interest in the team continued to decline. Despite the efforts of the Chattanooga Jaycees and other civic leaders to stimulate public support, questions of non-payment of the small player salaries raised the question of whether the team would finish the season and play any road trip games in September.

In an effort to create more public support, Charles O. Ragan announced in November 1965, that he was negotiating with the Kansas City Chiefs in the American Football League to establish a working agreement as a minor league franchise for the Cherokees. Unfortunately, no formal relationship ever materialized.

Howard Sompayac, the new Cherokee President, in September announced an intention to finish the 1965 season, but he pointed out that the team had not been paid for the last two weeks before the game against Columbus, Georgia, at the Rossville High School Field.

Former U.C. player and future Red Bank High School Coach, Tom Weathers, dropped off the team amid unconfirmed reports that several other players would do the same because of lack of pay.

In June 1966, the team hoped for a brighter future in the North American Football League after the Southern Football League collapsed after the 1965 season.

The coaching staff for 1966 was announced as Vic Varney; Cotton Letner; and former Central, Auburn, and San Francisco Forty Niner player, Bobby Hoppe, who had played for the Cherokees in 1965.

By this time owner Charles O. Ragan had delegated most of his authority to subordinates as his dream for a successful semi-pro team in Chattanooga evaporated when the NAFL discontinued operations after the 1966 season.

From 1962-1966 the Chattanooga Cherokees provided an opportunity for former high school and college players to once again put on the football pads and briefly return to the days of former successful careers amid limited and dwindling fan and financial support.

Chattanooga's Roller Derby Skaters

When Chicago sports promoter, Leo Seltzer, invented the banked oval track sport of "Roller Derby" in 1930, he created a popular source of entertainment that competed with wrestling at the Memorial Auditorium in Chattanooga for the attention of local sports fans.

During the 1930's-1973 era, competing teams from Chicago, California, and other parts of the country would fill the auditorium on a yearly tour that usually lasted a week at the local venue.

Joan Weston, known as the "Blonde Bomber", "Blonde Amazon", and "Golden Girl" was the recognized queen of the Roller Derby during the era as a member of the San Francisco Bay Bombers. A talented athlete in several sports, the 5 foot 10 inch, 165 pound blonde Weston loomed over the smaller participants, and she was the recognized star on the roller derby circuit. She replaced Annie "Big Red" Jensen as the Bay Bombers captain in 1965.

Combining athletic skills with rough house tactics, including tripping, hair pulling, and throwing opposing players over the ring rails surrounding the oval track, the derby attracted contact-oriented fans in the traditions of wrestling and stock car racing.

The purported creation of bitter rivalries between star skaters such as Weston and villain, "Demon of the Derby," Ann Calvello, further stimulated fan interest. The feuds in the ring not only were bitter, but they were also personal. Blue collar and beer drinking fans throughout the country made Roller Derby a leading spectator sport during the period.

Aroused audiences would retaliate against Calvello and other villains that were on each team by throwing objects at the skaters or attacking them as they left the ring. What Leo Seltzer envisioned being a relatively tame competition changed into a more violent sport when sports writer, Damon Runyon, helped Leo rewrite the rules that increased violence – and attendance. Very few matches did not include illegal kicks and punches that sometimes exceeded the theatrical and resulted in serious injuries. Twisted arms, knee injuries, broken collarbones, and loss of teeth were all common occurrences.

Most of the female skaters had nicknames. The most prominent were Midge "Toughie" Brasham and Loretta "Little Iodine" Behrens.

Movie stars such as W.C. Fields, Mickey Rooney, Cary Grant, George Burns, Gracie Allen, and Eddie Cantor held reserved box seats at Hollywood's Pen Pacific Auditorium in 1953, and the Los Angeles Braves attracted a crowd of sixty thousand fans in a match in the Rose Bowl.

A little known fact is that many Chattanoogans were represented in the roller derby by Betty "Little Red" Boyd as a member of the Jersey Jolters. In December, 1944, she participated in tryouts in Chattanooga along with future Hall of Fame member, Mary Lou "Lulu" Palermo, of Chicago. In 1946 she married fellow skater, Bob Satterfield, and they had a daughter Donna, who at age 2 traveled with her mother to matches across the country.

In a recent telephone interview with Lulu she related that Chattanooga always opened the yearly Roller Derby season on December 26. She surmised that the Scenic City was chosen because of its role as a railroad hub with lines to all points of the country. After Chattanooga, the teams would travel by train to Houston and Fort Worth, Texas, and continue to Florida for the winter season.

According to Ms. Palermo, several skaters prominent in roller derby from Chattanooga including Red Smartt, Betty Boyd, June Brock, Robby Burns, Edith Branum, Peggy Smalley, Rita Bush, George Bolt, and Jack Wilson. While many of the skaters have passed, the survivors still stay in touch with each other and have a reunion each year in May in Las Vegas, Nevada.

Other recognized male stars in the sport were Ken Monte and William "Red" Smartt, who joined the Roller Derby in Chattanooga in 1947. Two years later, Smartt would be elevated to the position of captain of the Chicago Westerners. He was crowned Roller Derby "King" in 1955 and was selected for the All Star Team from 1954-1959.

Roller Derby was one of the first sports to be televised in 1946, and while black-and-white television helped to prolong the life of the bank track derby, the sport eventually succumbed to skater's strikes, the gasoline crisis in the 1970's. Increased operational costs eventually put the original Roller Derby league out of business after its last match on December 3, 1973.

Prior to its demise, Seltzer's son, Jerry, moved the Los Angeles team to the San Francisco Bay area and eventually syndicated the sport to 120 television stations throughout the nation.

Although the sport has received some rejuvenation with women flat track games, it has not acquired the prominence that it once held in the days of the National Roller Derby. Chattanooga now has a women's team, the Chattanooga Roller Derby, that was formed in 2008. They play their home games at the Chattanooga Convention Center.

Roller Derby photo courtesy of UTC

Chattanooga's Contributors to Stock Car Racing History

With the passing of Harold E. Fryar, Jr. on November 16, 2015, the Chattanooga area lost another member of what was once a popular weekend past-time on the short dirt and asphalt race tracks in southeast Tennessee and northwest Georgia.

Harold Fryar, Sr. was just one of many well-known racers from this area during the early NASCAR era of races at sites such as Daytona, Talladega, Bristol, etc. He was inducted posthumously into the Georgia Racing Hall of Fame in 2015.

Harold and Freddy Fryar, Raymond "Friday" Hassler, Joe Lee Johnson, Bobby Burcham and Grant Adcock are a few of the local drivers who raced, won, and sometimes died in the races prior to the development of NASCAR into prominence on the big tracks.

Robert Richey driving "The Rolling Donut" vehicle, named after his family's donut shop at the top of McCallie Avenue in the Highland Park area, is remembered as the winner of a "backwards race" at Warner Park on the old horse racing track. His family has continued to participate in stock car racing.

Warner Park, Alton Park (Chattanooga Speedway), Soddy Daisy, Cleveland and East Ridge all had dirt tracks that held regular races on the weekends. Most of the drivers were amateurs who worked regular jobs during the week while preparing their cars for the weekend. Boyd Speedway outside East Ridge has undergone several changes in ownership over the years, but it still provides an outlet for racers of this generation.

Lake Winnepesaukah, under the direction of owner and founder, Carl Dixon, also had a dirt track that adjoined the lake. Carl was also an expert driver during the 1920's-1940's at the facility, but he retired from racing to participate in the development of the popular northwest Georgia tourist attraction outside Rossville. He had previously competed at the old horse-racing track at Warner Park, and in 1921, while driving a Hassler Special car, he won the twenty-five mile race during the Chattanooga Interstate Fair. Dixon was described as a "fearless" driver.

Freddy Fryar, known as "the Beaumont Flyer," is Harold's younger brother and started his racing career in Chattanooga at the age of fourteen in the 1950's. Although Harold Fryar, Sr. died in an accident on a one-half mile track in 1971, Freddy carried on the family tradition.

Freddy, during his career won seven NASCAR Series Track Championships and three state championships in Texas, Louisiana and Mississippi. After he retired from racing, he became an instructor at Richard Petty's driving school for several years. In 2012-2013 he was inducted into the Georgia, Alabama, and Ozarks Racing Halls of Fame in recognition of his 826 victories during a period of thirty-seven years.

Raymond "Friday" Hassler, who died in a crash at Daytona Beach in 1972 while qualifying during his first Daytona 500 at the age of 36, was one of the most prominent racers during 1960-1972. His most significant victory was at Bristol Motor Speedway during the 1971 Volunteer 500 when he was a relief driver for the eventual winner, Charlie Glotzback. He was steadily moving up the ranks as a driver, and his unfortunate death cut short the potential for a successful career in NASCAR. Hassler is credited with participating in 135 races during a ten-year period.

Joe Lee Johnson was another popular racer and owner of the Cleveland Tennessee Speedway. He was the first winner of the World 600 (now Coca-Cola 600) at Charlotte, North Carolina, and the previous year had won NASCAR's convertible division. Johnson is prominently mentioned in a 2014 history of racing, *A History of East Tennessee Auto Racing*, written by David McGee.

Robert Wayne "Bob" Burcham was known as the "Bullet from Rossville, Georgia" in racing during the 1950's-1970's when he participated in stock car racing. He was honored for his accomplishments by being inducted into the Tennessee and Georgia Racing Hall of Fame. Burcham raced in the Winston Cup Series and finished in the "top ten" on several occasions. His best finish was fourth place in a race in Nashville, Tennessee, in 1974. He died in April, 2009, at the age of seventy-three.

The brilliant NASCAR career of Herbert Grant Adcock ended at the age of thirty-nine on November 19, 1989, at a fatal crash in the Atlanta Journal 500 Winston Cup Series in a single car accident. Grant had started racing in 1974 under the sponsorship of his family's Chevrolet dealership in Chattanooga.

However, Grant's death from an improperly mounted racing seat led to new safety regulations as to how seats would be mounted in the future. Adcock was dominant in the ARCA class of competition that utilized older Winston Cup cars. ARCA's sportsmanship award, the H.G. Adcock Award, is awarded annually at two memorial races in north Georgia and Cleveland, Tennessee, that have been run in his memory.

Issues of safety have always been controversial in stock car racing. The idea of wearing safety equipment such as seat belts and flame retardant racing suits are just two of the many safety features added since the events started in the late 1940's-1950's. Driver resistance to many changes was common as many thought it distracted from the "manly" aspect of the sport. In fact the cars in the first Strictly Stock race at Charlotte Speedway in the 1940's were not even required to have roll bars or seat belts.

Safety advances in NASCAR have, with few exceptions, come as the result of tragic consequences. Every era can be defined by the safety improvements made during the period. In the '40's it was the adoption of crash helmets; in the '50's it was roll bars in the cars, and in the '60's it was the roll cage. When seat belts were made mandatory in the '50's several drivers protested and would not race, claiming it hindered their ability to escape from their cars after a wreck.

The defiant attitude lessened significantly on February 18, 2001, when superstar, Dale Earnhardt, was killed in a crash in the last lap of the Daytona 500 as the result of a "basilar skull fracture" caused by a whiplash in a relatively minor accident.

The death of Dale Earnhardt accelerated NASCAR's revolution. The adoption of several mandatory safety measures may have also saved NASCAR as a sport and avoided potential legislative action by Congress to control or ban the racing forum.

These pioneers and others in the field of stock car racing in our area have provided the inspiration for young people to aspire to become drivers in the highly popular and competitive NASCAR industry. However, most will continue to race on the dirt and asphalt in the area for the pleasure of competing and the thrill of victory.

Wrestling or "Rassling" in Chattanooga

The Soldiers and Sailors Memorial Auditorium, built between 1922-1924, to honor area Veterans of World War I, has over the years provided entertainment to the many wrestling or "rassling" fans in Hamilton County and Northwest Georgia.

Although the facility has hosted religious festivals, opera, the Cotton Ball for débutantes, musical concerts and political rallies for George Wallace and others during its ninety-two year existence, no activity has been more popular than the Saturday night "wrestling-rassling" cards put on by promoters, Nick Gulas, Ray Welch and Harry Thornton during the 1950's – 1980's.

Prior to the advent of the World Wrestling Federation and cable television, Memorial Auditorium held matches that included many of the national stars of the sport such as Gorgeous George; world champions, Lou Thesz, Verne Gagne and Andre the Giant, as well as many lesser known younger combatants.

Nick Gulas and Roy Welch owned the exclusive wrestling contacts for the entire South and employed Harry Thornton to be their local announcer for the matches. This also led to a Saturday afternoon television match at WRGP Channel 3, which at that time was located across from Warner Park on McCallie Avenue. Harry's studio show was later moved to WDEF TV Channel 12.

Although the Memorial Auditorium was supposedly limited by the fire marshals to allow it to hold no more than 3,866 fans, this number was often exceeded by the rabid supporters who came to cheer the "good guys" and boo the "villains."

The roles of the "wrestlers-rasslers" often switched over the weeks as the promoters strived to entertain the audiences. A "good guy" would suddenly be transformed into a "villain" when they suddenly pulled some unethical or illegal tactic on a less talented opponent, referee, or some fan in the audience who had been planted there to take the physical abuse.

The ability of the participants to stimulate the cheering (and booing) of the fans often overflowed to those sitting on the front rows outside the ring.

The use of bobby pins propelled by rubber bands by excited female fans and striking the bodies of the performers was not uncommon.

The ability of Gorgeous George to incite the audience by prancing around in his purple robe, dyed blonde hair with golden bobby pins, while his valet sprayed perfume on him and the audience, are part of the local wrestling-rassling history.

Legitimate wrestlers such as Lou Thesz, Ken Rossi and Verne Gagne tangled with villains such as Tojo Yamamoto, who actually was of Hawaiian descent, not Japanese. However he possessed the ability to irritate the national sentiments of the local citizens with his purported allegiance to Japan. He was frequently attacked by female fans who struck him with their purses as he entered or exited the arena.

Perennial women's World Champion Mildred Berke and her successor, the flamboyant and often irritating, The Fabulous Moolah, usually prevailed in the matches between the not-so-gentle fairer sex. Hair pulling and unsuccessful efforts to expose the anatomy of the opponent also led to the excitement of the moment.

Other crowd pleasing events included tag team events where one wrestler was in danger of being pinned when his partner came to his rescue by illegally breaking up the match and ending it by the touching of the shoulders on the mat for a three count.

Masked villains, who agreed to take off their mask and leave town if they lost, often stimulated attendance for several Saturdays as opponents unsuccessfully attempted to defeat the masked participants. Local banker, Arch Howell, III, vividly recalls as a young boy the excitement of seeing the white clad, "Medics," embarrassed when their masks had to come off after a defeat.

"Rassle Royals," where several individuals competed against each other to try and be the sole survivor, also were special events that kept the crowds returning to Memorial Auditorium.

The incomparable Harry Thornton had the talent to promote the sport as both a ring announcer and early a.m. host of the sport on the "The Morning Show" on Channel 12. The show went on the air in 1969 and finally ended on July 2, 1982. Over the years, he had several female co-hostesses that began with Ruth Boyer and ended with Judy Corn. On occasion, Harry's wife, Helen, who acquired the nickname "Mrs. T", would be the guest hostess, and the on air exchanges between her and her husband further helped the show's ratings. The program maintained its number-one rating for many years with its controversial discussion on local politics. The host and hostesses accepted calls from anonymous citizens, which often heightened interest and unfounded rumors on the show.

The last reported wrestling matches and events held at the Memorial Auditorium took place on October 10, 1983, when a relative unknown participant, Brett Wayne, won over an equally unknown Jake Roberts by disqualification.

Irrespective of whether it was real wrestling or fake "rassling," it was strongly supported in this area prior to its being replaced by the national cable television extravaganzas. It continues today on a smaller scale at several area locales in Tennessee and Georgia.

"Wrestling-Rassling" provided a source of inexpensive entertainment for thousands of loyal local fans who relished the antics of the men and women who climbed into the ring at the Memorial Auditorium.

Harry Thornton interviews "Pretty Boy" Michael Hayes and Terry Gordy for Channel 12 TV. Photo by Scott Teal.

The Soap Box Derby
Chattanooga's Non-Motorized NASCAR

The past and present history of the National Soap Box Derby has a strong Chattanooga connection.

What started as an idea by a *Dayton* (Ohio) *Daily News* photographer named Myron E. (Scottie) Scott in 1933, has evolved into an international event for youngsters interested in non-motorized racing.

The first race was held in 1934 in Dayton, with a variety of homemade vehicles involved in the inaugural contest. Thirty-four cities were represented, including Chattanooga. Scott, using his connections in the newspaper industry, had acquired the backing and support of local papers as major sponsors.

The *Chattanooga Times* strongly supported the initial race, and local automobile dealers Newton Chevrolet and Hamilton Chevrolet were co-sponsors with the *Times*.

Preliminary races began on August 2, 1934. The original race site was scheduled to be on the west side of the tunnel onto McCallie Avenue. Unfortunately, due to the high slope, the route caused some accidents to occur, and the decision was made to transfer the event to a gentler downward angle. Wilcox Boulevard on the eastern side of the Wilcox Tunnel was selected, and the race continued without any future mishaps.

Another race location was "Big 9" (now Martin Luther King, Jr. Boulevard). The starting line was at the crest of Main Street near Park Avenue with the young racers proceeding downhill in a westward direction into the heart of the African-American business district.

A total of 60 homemade vehicles participated in the first race down Wilcox Boulevard.

Chattanooga's first local winner and representative to the race in Dayton was Claude Alexander, Jr. of Signal Mountain. Although the Chattanoogan had the fastest times in his "Flash No.1" racer, under the handicap system that was used based on their speeds in earlier time trials, he was the runner-up. Young Claude completed the course in 55.2 seconds, but with a 4.5 second handicap, he finished 1.3 seconds behind the winner, Robert Turner, of Muncie, Indiana. Turner won the title of "All American Soap Box Racing Champion" and a four year college scholarship. Claude Alexander's second place finish earned him a trip to the Century of Progress Exposition (World's Fair) in Chicago, Illinois.

A large crowd of 50,000 fans viewed the first soap box derby. Ironically, no specific record exists as to whether a soapbox was ever actually used in the construction of a racer.

A controversy arose in the 1934 races in both Chattanooga and Dayton over the use of roller or ball bearings in the wheels. Due to an ambiguity in the official rule book, it was eventually decided to allow racers to use either type of bearing to participate.

The races continued to be held until they were discontinued during World War II in 1941–1946. The contest returned to Ninth Street until 1949, and the sponsorship of the event had been taken up by the *Chattanooga Times-Free Press* when Y.L. Coker, Jr. was the local winner.

A hiatus period of inactivity continued until 1976 when the races were reactivated under the leadership of the Chattanooga Kiwanis Club. A track was set up on Fourth Street near the YMCA, and the races headed downhill in an eastern direction near the freeway entrance.

In 1935, the national Derby moved to Akron, Ohio, at a site named Talmadge Hill. It has remained in Akron since that year, and in 1936, "Derby Downs" was constructed near the Akron Municipal Airport where the races continue to be held.

Chevrolet became the main major sponsor until 1972 when John Z. Delorean became Chevy's division general manager, and he discontinued the automobile manufacturer's financial support. Local organizations such as the Akron Chamber of Commerce and Jaycees came to the rescue, and the Derby has continued and expanded to this day.

More regulation, female participation, and required uniform part kits are just a few of the changes that have occurred over the years.

Like NASCAR, the Kentucky Derby, or any other type of race, cheating has been detected.

In 1973, a young racer from Boulder, Colorado, was stripped of his title after it was discovered that an electromagnet had been installed in the nose of his car. When the driver leaned backwards at the starting line, his metal helmet activated a battery power source. When the electricity flowed through the steel ramp used to start the race, the car surged forward. A two-day investigation resulted in the youngster's disqualification, and his uncle was charged with contributing to the delinquency of a minor. The uncle paid restitution in the amount of $2,000 to the Boys' Club of Boulder.

In Chattanooga, the race moved to a course at the Hamilton County landfill in 1977 in Harrison off Birchwood Pike and was held at that location until 1983. Soap Box Derby eventually fell into decline and was discontinued for a period of twenty years.

In 2008, a young lawyer and former participant in the Derby from his original hometown, Roanoke, Virginia, resurrected the Chattanooga Soap Box Derby. Michael Stewart, a practicing attorney at Chambliss, Bahner and Stophel, became the director and reactivated the historic event each summer.

With the help of Hamilton County Commissioner Larry Henry, the Hamilton County Parks and Recreation Department, the Tennessee Department of Transportation, and a large group of volunteers, Derby Downs at the Redoubt Soccer Complex off Bonnie Oaks Drive has continued to this date under the enthusiastic leadership of Michael Stewart.

Primarily, carrying the financial and organizational load by himself, Stewart's dream of many a youngster being a contestant in its qualifying races, with the hope of qualifying for the big race in Akron, have been fulfilled under Michael's leadership.

The second major revival of the race took place in 2009, and local kids competed at the new race course at the Redoubt Soccer Complex. In addition to Claude Alexander, Jr., Chattanoogans Will Suggs in 1977, Amy Higgins in 1982, and Ray Hixson in 1982 have finished second in their class in Akron. The grandfather of a 2015 local participant, Charlie Hooks, was the national winner in 1949 from his hometown of Charleston, West Virginia.

Chattanooga continues to be represented at Akron each July, but in a quite different vehicle from the one Claude Alexander, Jr. drove in 1934. In 2015, Lucas Johnson and Jessica Little carried the Chattanooga banner to the national championship in Ohio during a week in July. The event has continued to grow, and boys and girls compete in three different size cars: stock, super stock, and master stock cars.

Uniform part kits are purchased from the national organization for kids aged 7–17. Parts are strictly regulated, but allow some flexible individual creativity. Additional information is available on the national organization's website at www.aasbd.org.

In 2017, thirteen-year-old driver Ashton Stevenson achieved the highest finish of any local driver to date when she finished third out of one hundred and twenty cars in the Super car category. In 2019 national races were again held in Akron, Ohio, and eleven-year-old Chase Stewart and thirteen-year-olds Parker Stewart and Jessica Little represented Chattanooga, with Parker finishing third in the Challenge race. Also, in 2019, the local association held a Thanksgiving Invitational race and cars from twenty-one states participated. Two were from the State of Washington, and there were also entries from California, Connecticut and Florida. The 2020 All American Race in Akron, Ohio, was canceled due to the Corona virus pandemic.

Individuals and groups interested in sponsoring, building, and racing in the 2021 Chattanooga season should contact Director Michael Stewart at (423) 596-7726 or (423) 757-0282 to help continue this race's historical legacy.

Soap Box Derby in Chattanooga in 1940

Sewanee Football
SEC to Division III

Much has been written about the 1899 undefeated football team that scored 322 total points versus all their opponents' total of 10 points.

Their remarkable feat of winning five games in six days away from home earned the squad the title as the "greatest football team of all-time" in 2012 by the College Football Hall of Fame, and the moniker "Iron Men of Sewanee." The opponents that were demolished were Texas (12-0), Texas A&M (10-0), Tulane (23-0), LSU (34-0), and Ole Miss (12-0). Seven other victories were claimed against other foes with all of them being shut out completely except Auburn (11-10). They scored the only opposing 10 points for the entire year.

Sewanee had first fielded a football team in 1891 and dominated collegiate football until the larger schools began subsidizing athletes. In 1924, Sewanee joined the Southern Conference, the SEC's predecessor, and only had one season where the squad won more games than it lost. In 1932, Sewanee was a founding or charter member of the Southeastern Conference (SEC) along with ten schools which included Alabama, Auburn, Florida, Georgia, Kentucky, LSU, Mississippi, Mississippi State, Tennessee and Vanderbilt, with Tulane and Georgia Tech later playing in the Atlantic Coast Conference (ACC).

Sewanee, a small school with around two hundred students, quickly fell behind the other schools who were beginning to spend large sums of money on athletes, particularly football. On September 30, 1933, the Purple Tigers visited the University of Kentucky for the first football game in the newly formed SEC. The score was 7-0 in favor of the Wildcats. Except for a 10-6 loss to Florida in 1938 things never got better.

From its entry into the SEC from 1933-1940, Sewanee lost all thirty-seven of its games on a non-home field basis, as road games were more financially lucrative compared to the little school on the mountain. During its membership in the SEC, the school's aggregate score was opponents 1,163 points – Sewanee 84 points. Sewanee probably would have never joined the SEC except for the pressure put on the school by and avid alumni and the widely respected Bishop Frank Juhan, a College

Football Hall of Famer who was a graduate of Sewanee and who loved both the school and the sport of football.

Sewanee's historical tradition, influential alumni, and financial supporters prevented the school from accepting reality that there was no benefit of being in the SEC, and the prospect of competing with the larger universities would continue to be a disaster. Finally, in 1938, with the vice-chancellor Benjamin Ficklin Finney on his way out, the university turned to former Baylor School president and president of the University of Chattanooga, Alexander Guerry, to address the issue of Sewanee's continued membership in the SEC. Guerry conditioned his coming to Sewanee on the elimination of scholarship athletes.

In 1940, Sewanee withdrew from the SEC and would eventually become a member of what is now the NCAA's Division III. Loud protests came from alumni, fans and former players. Perhaps the biggest outcry came after the loss of the traditional Sewanee-Vanderbilt game on Thanksgiving Day in Nashville. The rivalry began in 1902, and through the 1920's, was the Southeast's great ritual. For twenty-eight consecutive Turkey Days, the Commodores and Tigers had met. The largest crowd was a near capacity one in 1922, but by 1929 the crowds had dwindled to 7,000 fans, and Vanderbilt finally pulled the plug on the game in 1931.

This action created a severe financial loss on Sewanee as this was its main revenue game. Thus ended the historical contest between the two schools which, with a few exceptions, has achieved mediocrity for both Vanderbilt in the SEC Division, and Sewanee in Division III. However, both have retained their reputations of being excellent institutions of academics in America.

Though mostly played against schools with players only having non-athletic scholarship programs, there have still been seasons of outstanding records. Under Coach Shirley Majors, the Tigers in 1958 and 1963 were undefeated in the Collegiate Athletic Conference (CAC), and in 2000 they won a share of the Southern Collegiate Athletic Conference (SCAC) for a total of thirteen conference titles in various conferences since the school left the SEC.

EVENTS

The Cotton Ball (1933-2020)

In 1933, the Late Zella A. Armstrong was the prime force in creating the yearly Cotton Ball in Chattanooga. The Ball became the premier "coming out" of young ladies primarily from Hamilton County and surrounding communities.

It was a lavish weeks-long celebration with many teas, parties, and luncheons presented by the parents and others for the débutantes from many of the Chattanooga area's most prominent families. The selection and announcement of a young queen and successful older king was the highlight of the event that took place usually at the Memorial Auditorium amongst elegant surroundings carefully orchestrated by the event founder, Miss Armstrong. Lovely young ladies in beautiful gowns, dashing young men in coat and tail tuxedos were presented to the adoring audience of proud parents and friends amidst a back drop of pageantry reminiscent of the splendor of the Old South.

Zella Armstrong was a spinster from a southern family dating back to the Civil War. Her father, John M. Armstrong, was a young lieutenant in the Confederate Army in June 1862, and he commanded the canon that returned fire when Federal troops first shelled Chattanooga. Born around 1872 (she never revealed her age), her love of history, tradition, and love of the South inspired Zella to become the originator of the first Cotton Ball in 1933.

A published author and one of the earliest female reporters, she was one of the founders and a former president of the Tennessee Women's Press Club. Her list of occupations included editor, poet, and author of numerous genealogical sketches and papers, several volumes of *Notable Southern Families* published by Lookout Publishing Company, playwriting, and she was the Hamilton County Historian appointed by County Judge Will Cummings.

In 1940, Chattanooga Mayor Ed Bass presented Miss Armstrong with a silver medal identifying her as, "Chattanooga's Number 1 Woman

Citizen" in recognition of her, "loving her city, state, her nation and her Southland, with fervor and a constancy that few could boast."

The overwhelming majority of débutantes that were fortunate enough to be presented as Queen, or members of the Court, credit Zella Armstrong with instilling the same qualities of service and philanthropy that helped them to grow into productive parents and members of the community. The same has to be true of the Kings and young men who escorted the ladies on the night of the coronation. Most of them have also served as leaders in the city, county, state, and nation.

When she died on April 12, 1965, while confined to a nursing home, she still directed the operation of *The Lookout*, a journal of social and historical items that for years appeared in the *Chattanooga Times Free-Press* on a weekly basis.

Her legacy continues today with the annual Cotton Ball continuing its tradition of recognition and selection of outstanding young ladies to be presented at the gala event and who mostly grow into the leaders of philanthropy in our community.

However, in deference to changing times and social mores, the leadership of the Junior League has voted to remove the word "Cotton" from its name in 2020 and to rename the event "The Chattanooga Ball."

It is doubtful that Zella Armstrong would approve.

Miss Zella Armstrong and Mayor Ed Bass before Cotton Ball queen Virginia Guild in 1938

Tennessee Adoption Scandal

This article was initiated by a call and question from a listener on Judy O'Neal's cable television show, *Town Talk,* in Fort Oglethorpe, Georgia, on January 16, 2020.

The Tennessee Children's Home Society, based in Memphis with branches in Jackson, Knoxville and Chattanooga, was created as a non-profit corporation in 1897. Later its head was Georgia Tann, who with her political connections in the Tennessee General Assembly, and the local Shelby County political head, Edward Crump (The Red Snapper), and Shelby County Family Court Judge, Camille Kelley, operated a "baby for sale" adoption agency that became a national recognized organization that would later become a national scandal.

Misguided community organizations supported the concept of placing orphaned and unwanted children in homes of families desiring to adopt them. This noble purpose quickly turned into a lucrative money-making scheme until 1950, following a state investigation into its illegal practices.

The Society, headed by Tann, was simply a black-market adoption scheme which sold babies to adopting parents throughout America. These included movie stars in Hollywood. Actresses Lana Turner and Joan Crawford adopted children through the agency, and June Allison and her husband, Dick Powell, also adopted a child from Tann. Professional wrestler, Ric Flair, in his autobiography, claimed that he had been illegally taken form his natural mother and sold through the Society to his adoptive parents.

Up until 1966, when Tennessee enacted adoption laws that allowed adopted adults to search any remaining records in an effort to locate their birth parents, such attempts were futile. Records were routinely destroyed, and many of Tann's infants to this day have not been able to identify their natural parents.

Even in 1941, when the Society lost its national endorsement from the Child Welfare League of America because of its practice of destroying adoption records, Tann remained wealthy in the for-profit business through her political connections with the Tennessee Legislature.

It was only after a 1950 state investigation of the Society, initiated by Governor Gordon Browning, that he released a scalding report implicating Judge Camille Kelley and Tann. Kelley was never prosecuted, although she lived a lifestyle well beyond the salary of a Family Court Judicial Officer. She did resign shortly after the release of the 1950 report.

Tann allegedly made millions from the sale of babies. She drove a Packard or Cadillac automobile and dressed in expensive clothes. She would die from a stroke on January 28, 1955. Tann started at the Mississippi Children Home Funding Society around 1920 and initially placed orphans for adoption, but she quickly realized she could charge hefty fees for placing children who had been kidnapped from poor women.

In 1924, she started working at the Tennessee Children's Home Society where she turned part-time baby snatching into a highly profitable business. For about 30 years, she developed a network of corrupt judges, politicians and scouts who would help her, in essence, steal babies. Youngsters on the way home from school would be kidnapped by offering the children ice cream.

Some victims were sold throughout the United States, Britain and other countries as underage farm hands. Reports of the children being enslaved, beaten or raped by pedophiles were widespread. Unfortunately, Tann's phony credibility allowed her to be praised in the national press as "the foremost authority on its adoption laws."

First lady Eleanor Roosevelt reached out to Tann for advice regarding child welfare, and she was invited to President Truman's 1948 inauguration. Tann would die from cancer in 1950 before the circumstances of the scandal were fully disclosed to the public.

A "Report to Governor Gordon Browning on Shelby County Branch, Tennessee Children's Home Society" 1951 [Nashville]: State of Tennessee, Department of Public Welfare" contains the history and details of the Tennessee Adoption Scandal. In 1991, CBS's "60 Minutes" reported on the scandal, and it stimulated laws to open adoption records by both birth mothers and adoptees. The Tennessee Children's Home Society was closed in 1950 and should not be confused with the modern-day ministry known as Tennessee Children's Home, which is accredited by the State of Tennessee.

Copperhill – McCaysville Adoption Scandal

In the previous story, we discussed the Tennessee Adoption Scandal that originated in Memphis and involved a high priced adoptions criminal enterprise led by Georgia Tann. On a much smaller scale a similar adoption scandal, that also included illegal abortions, occurred in the small towns of Copperhill, Tennessee, and the McCaysville, Georgia, area between 1950 and early 1960s.

Thomas Hicks was born on October 18, 1888, and received his medical degree from the Emory University, Atlanta, in 1917. As a county doctor serving the two mining communities on the Tennessee-Georgia state lines, Dr. Hicks had a Dr. Jekyll-Mr. Hyde existence.

His Dr. Jekyll persona as the congenial and friendly county doctor also included performing illegal abortions when young couples made a "mistake" and did not want to have a child or get married. This practice was tolerated by the community, and he normally was allegedly paid about $100 to perform the illegal practice.

Dr. Hicks was, "Considered a cornerstone in the Copperhill-McCaysville community where he served as the town doctor."

In treating some unwed mothers or women wanting to terminate their pregnancies, Hicks would pay special attention to them and would help them to stay at a hotel down the street from his clinic. He would also convince them to carry their babies to full term on the pretense that he would find good adoptive parents and provide the children with good homes.

However, he had another objective for urging that the babies be born. He would often tell the natural mother that the child was stillborn and was deceased at birth. Dr. Hicks would then sell the babies for $800 to $1000 each. He would provide a forged birth certificate with the adoptive parents on the documents, but no reference was made of the real mother.

He soon developed a clandestine reputation of a physician who could provide a baby for adoption. It was reported that at least 49 of the babes were sold to couples in the Akron, Ohio, area. During the 1950s through early 1960s, he allegedly sold more than 200 newborn children through his Hicks Community Clinic in Copperhill-McCaysville.

In spite of the illegal practices of selling babies and performing abortions in the two states, he was never charged criminally with either of these offenses. However, he was found guilty of illegally selling narcotic pain killers and of income tax invasion. He served time in federal prison. In 1964 he surrendered his medical license for performing an illegal abortion.

He allegedly died of leukemia at the age of 83 on March 5, 1972. The secret of the baby-for-sale scandal lay pretty much unknown until around 1997. Since then, and with the successful development of DNA evidence, many adopted babies now in their 50s – 70s have been able to reconnect with their natural parents. Known as the "Hicks Babies," several have been able to find out the truth about their past. It has come too late for others, as their real parents have died.

The television program "Nightline" spoke with several people who have found out they were Hicks Babies. The program assisted them to provide DNA samples with the genealogy website Ancestry.com who has the capacity to compare over 700,000 DNA matches using the latest advanced technology. Some matches were successful; others were not.

Thus, the legacy of Dr. Thomas Hicks remains an unanswered mystery of many residents in the dual border towns of Copperhill-McCaysville. Numerous Google sites display heart wrenching stories about this unfortunate period in both small town histories.

Dr. Thomas Hicks

Chattanooga's Divorce Mill Scandal

Perhaps the darkest historical period of injustice in Hamilton County occurred during World War II and involved many soldiers that were stationed at Fort Oglethorpe. Georgia. The *Chattanooga Times* had previously made editorial comments criticizing the way that "quickie" divorces were granted in the county to the extent that the area was often referred to as the "Reno, Nevada of the South."

Finally the Chattanooga Bar Association (CBA) appointed a committee under the chairmanship of attorney Clarence Kolwyck to study the matter, because the nature of the charges "seriously reflected against the bar as a whole." Part of the committee's finding was that the situation was partially caused by the proximity of Hamilton County to the State of Georgia, which was described as, "A state with lax marriage laws."

The inquiry as to any alleged illegalities in the handling of divorces was initiated by an article on the front page of the *Chattanooga Times* by reporter Vaughn Smartt on February 10, 1946. His story was based on a suit by a recently discharged soldier who, upon returning to Hamilton County, had discovered that he had not been given any notice of the divorce as required by the Soldiers and Sailors Relief Act under federal law. The soldier asked for a refund from his wife of funds allotted to her during the time he was overseas fighting for his country, because she had obtained a divorce without his knowledge.

Mr. Smartt, as an investigative reporter, checked the Circuit Court docket and discovered that there were nine pending cases for disposition where the same law firm was representing both the wife and husband in their divorce. Upon the filing of the petition for divorce, a lawyer sharing offices with the attorney who filed the petition was appointed as a guardian to represent the soldier. Usually within four-five days, an answer would be filed submitting the soldier's interest to the court, and the wife would be awarded the military allotment, insurance death benefits or other items sought from the unknowing and absent soldier.

As a result of Mr. Smartt's articles, Chattanooga Bar Association President Gus A. Wood, Jr. appointed a five-member committee headed by Clarence Kolwyck and included William G. Brown, William F. Clark, John J. Lively, Jr., and Harry Weill. A study of the divorces granted from

1945-1947 revealed numerous irregularities on at least thirteen different grounds that could possibly affect the validity of the divorces.

Although several attorneys were involved in the illegal granting of divorces, only two were selected to have disciplinary action imposed by the courts against them. The older member of the two-man firm involved in several of the illegal divorces accepted a two-year suspension of his law license and immediately retired from the practice of law. His younger guilty colleague also received a two-year suspension and became a teacher at a local high school teaching social studies and civics. After his retirement as a teacher, he would be allowed to regain his law license. He primarily handled appointed cases in his later years.

The committee reported that, for the calendar year 1945, twenty-nine hundred and six (2,906) divorce cases were filed in Hamilton County with 98.5% being assigned to one judge, which strongly suggests that the practice of "judge shopping" was prevalent. However, the report states. "It is not to be inferred from anything said herein that this committee impugn the motives of Judge Miller whom we all know to be the very soul of honor. He is truly the friend of everyone and desires the respect of all."

For "statistical purposes" the number of cases wherein a final decree of divorce was granted was reduced to 1,000 for study. A lengthy article of the proceedings is contained in Volume 19, Number 8, June 1947 of the Tennessee Law Review by Mr. Walter Garland, Instructor of Law, University of Tennessee College of Law. In twenty-seven pages, Garland discusses the marriage and divorce laws in Georgia and Tennessee, the statistical data involved in the survey from 1945-1947, and the recommended corrective action to protect parties in divorce actions in the future.

Times reporter Smartt was rewarded by the CBA for his discovery of the irregularities which precipitated the investigation by giving the *Times* the first release of the report for its Sunday edition. The initial release of the eight-four page committee report included twenty-five hundred (2,500) copies that were sent to all trial judges in Tennessee and other judges across the nation.

Clarence Kolwyck was elected as President of the CBA in 1947 and subsequently became President of the Tennessee Bar Association in 1956. The CBA was recognized nationally for its actions in addressing the problems in the marriage and divorce areas of the law in Tennessee

Moonshine Feud on Daisy Mountain

The rolling farm land, covered woods, and occasional waterfalls are part of a much quieter area of northern Hamilton County than what existed in 1947-1950.

Although the origin of the Parker/Ashley and Harris/Millsaps feud is often in dispute, it usually boils down to one of three theories.

Theodore "Pap" Parker was the head of the family that had manufactured and distributed moonshine in the county for many years. He allegedly purchased a house from Willie Harris in 1947, and he later found out that there was an existing mortgage on the property after Harris represented that it did not have any lien.

The second version of the origin of the bloody feud was that Harris was attempting to take over the moonshine industry in Hamilton County which Pap Parker had controlled for many years.

A third theory was that the troubles between the two family groups originated out of the hijacking of a load of illegal liquor.

The feud achieved local and national notoriety similar to the famous Hatfield and McCoy deadly quarrels in West Virginia and Kentucky.

During the administration of Hamilton County Sheriff Frank Burns (1948-1950), enforcement of the liquor laws against the manufacturing and sale of unstamped whiskey were not as vigorously prosecuted as some law-and-order supporters advocated.

However with the rare election of Republican Sheriff Rex Richey in 1950, the moonshiners were subjected to vigorous prosecutions. He had successfully campaigned upon, "A pledge of honest, courageous, and vigorous law enforcement." This attracted national attention including that of renowned radio personality, Arthur Godfrey.

During his first two years in office Richer allegedly destroyed 209 stills, 125,775 gallons of mash and 12,662 gallons of whiskey, with an estimated street value of $9,136,705.

Although the feud may have originated with the house-sale issue, it blossomed into murder and assault cases in 1948-1950, when four murders and fifteen felonious assaults occurred after the hijacking of a load of illegal liquor by one of the factions from the other. The first fatality occurred on September 19, 1948, nine months after the feud erupted, when twenty-six-year-old army veteran David Wilcox was ambushed in his convertible automobile, and his passenger, Willie Lee Harris, narrowly escaped with his life.

The second murder victim was George Trusley, who operated a restaurant and was killed on November 5, 1948, on the porch of his East Ridge, Tennessee, home. Trusley had a felonious assault charge, arising out of the moonshine feud, pending against him at the time of his death. Three members of the Harris clan, Joe Coleman, Harrison Leming, and Raymond Bell, were acquitted in Chattanooga in September, 1949, of the murder.

The third ambush victim during the feud was William L. "Boots" Parker, who was found lying on a muddy slope of Daisy Mountain after being shot three times and bludgeoned with an ax. Two brothers, Raymond and Ed Bell, were charged with Parker's murder.

Gunfire was subsequently directed towards Parker's supporters who had testified against the defendants at trial.

Pistol and rifle shots were directed towards the automobiles and homes of the two competing factions in that period of the feud.

"Pap" Parker and his wife, Ethel, had both sustained gunshot wounds during the feud. Mr. Parker was ambushed in the yard of his Daisy Mountain home and was hospitalized for several months. Mrs. Parker, a school teacher, claimed she still had a bullet in her head when a car in which she was riding was ambushed on September 7th.

Six sheriff deputies were sent out on special night patrol to stop the gangland attacks on Daisy Mountain.

When neighbors spied law enforcement officers on the mountain, they would fire two rifle shots as a warning of the presence of the sheriff deputies. On other occasions, the moonshiners would warn the local citizenry by blowing car horns, or women would sometimes bang tin pans.

At the time of the October, 1949, police action, neither Pap Parker nor Willie Harris were present in Hamilton County. Parker was serving an eighteen-month sentence in a federal prison in Kentucky for illegal manufacturing and distribution of moonshine. Harris had allegedly fled the area for his own safety and was rumored to be working in a Detroit, Michigan tire plant.

Criminal Judge Raulston Schoolfield, who had represented many of the participants in the feud prior to becoming elected in 1948, took direct action and revoked the bonds of all of those that had pending charges. He hoped to stop additional violence.

Harrison Leming, Joe Coleman, Mark Leming, and Tommy Frederick were initially convicted of one of the murders. Schoolfield granted them a new trial but would not give them a bond, and they remained in jail pending the retrial, at which time they were acquitted on July 14, 1949.

During December, 1948, the two warring factions made an unsuccessful attempt to resolve the continuous conflict on the national radio broadcast the "We the People" show by proclaiming an end to the feud.

However, it sporadically reoccurred. The rising price of sugar needed to manufacture moonshine, the cheaper cost of growing marijuana, and more sophisticated law enforcement methods, probably contributed much to the end of the "Daisy Mountain Moonshine Wars" in the 1940's-1950's.

Moonshine Feud on Daisy Mountain-No. 2

When Harry Mushegan (4/5/1918 – 5/8/2019) first accepted the position as pastor of the Daisy Church of God in the early 1950's, he did not know what type of community he was entering to serve the Lord.

Pastor Mushegan was a fearless man. Having grown up on the streets of Los Angeles, according to his daughter, Harolene Leguizamon, he himself had been involved in a street gang in California's largest city while a teenager. His "motorcycle group" was the East Los Angeles Falcons which later was adopted into the Hells Angels.

He was no stranger to groups trying to get rid of him. After he gave his life to God, he went into their territory in L.A. and pitched a tent to have a revival. On the first night of the services, the sounds of motorcycle motors became louder as he preached his sermon. The gang parked their bikes around the tent and then stood at each post outside. Pastor Mushegan kept preaching. Some of the gang members left, but a few of them stayed and came to the altar for salvation.

His daughter later repeated his comment, "It was his proudest moment."

Eventually he and his family would migrate to Daisy around 1952. He soon learned that the acknowledged head of one of the moonshine groups was "Pap" Parker and that his family attended the Daisy church.

Parker's wife, Ethel, was a schoolteacher who sometimes filled in as church pianist. Both she and Pap had sustained gunshot wounds in a moonshine feud. Pap was ambushed in the yard of his Daisy home and underwent medical treatment for several months. Mrs. Parker also claimed that she had a bullet in her head from when a car in which she was riding was ambushed.

When Pastor Mushegan first met Pap, the bootlegger told him that he had heard of him, that he was a good man, and that he had a piece of advice for him. "Preacher, while you are here, don't trade cars. These mountains are dangerous at night."

Pap offered to provide protection and gave an invitation to attend the homes of moonshiners so that he would be "welcomed" and recognized as a pastor and not be a rival of the group in the ongoing illegal liquor war.

During his tenure as pastor at Daisy Church of God, Pastor Mushegan performed at least two funerals a week during that time period.

His daughter later remarked again, "So much violence, yet so many good-hearted people."

Today the joint municipality of Soddy Daisy has shed its image of violence, but it has also continued its reputation of being full of "good-hearted" people!

Battle of Athens
McMinn County War

The returning ex-GIs from World War II little expected that they would fight another armed battle when they arrived back in McMinn County in 1946.

Political corruption and improper government had existed in Athens and Etowah for many years. Citizens' complaints of election fraud in 1940, 1942 and 1944 had gone unheeded with no action being taken by the United States Department of Justice after investigations.

In 1936, the Democratic candidate for sheriff from Etowah had won the office as part of the Roosevelt landslide across the county and established the political machines that would lead to the violence in the August, 1946, election.

McMinn County had a long history of bribe-taking by local politicians, the financing of the McMinn Sheriff by a fee system based on the amount of fines collected from often illegal arrests, and a pattern of voting fraud by both Democrats and Republicans.

Approximately 3,000 soldiers from McMinn County had fought in World War II. Many of them decided to get involved in the 1946 election in an effort to provide, "An honest ballot count and reform of county government."

They put forth a slate of political candidates in various offices that would oppose the political machine headed by the local sheriff, Pat Mansfield, and his colleague, Paul Cantrell, who had previously served as the chief law enforcement officer in the county, and who would again run in 1946 for sheriff.

In opposition, the community put forth an all ex-GI non-partisan ticket. The politicking became heated, and it became obvious that the threat of violence loomed over the upcoming August election.

In the local newspaper, the *Daily Post Athenian*, on June 17, 1946, one GI speaker said, "The principles that we fought for in this past war do not exist in McMinn County. We fought for democracy because we believe in democracy but not the forum we are under in this county."

In an effort to intimidate voters, (or keep down violence), Sheriff Mansfield swore in some 200 special deputies to oversee the election.

The most vivid historical depiction of the events of the election is described in a book by C. Stephen Bynum, *The Battle of Athens*, Parker Productions, Chattanooga, Tennessee, 1987.

As expected, violence erupted. One African-American voter was shot in the back; ex-GIs were fired upon, and the ballot boxes were seized by the sheriff's deputies and taken to the McMinn County jail for counting. This further enraged the citizens, and they placed the jail under siege with the sheriff and approximately 25 deputies inside.

In addition to their individual firearms, the GIs borrowed a set of keys to the National Guard and State Guard Armory and seized three M-1 rifles, five .45 semi-automatic pistols, and 24 British certified rifles.

Gun battles took place with varying dispositions. Estimates ranged from "a few rounds fired" up to "over 3000" as later described by participants and witnesses. Parties on both sides were wounded, and around 2:00 a.m. on August 2nd, GIs threw dynamite sticks onto the jail's porch causing substantial damage. The deputies immediately surrendered, and the GIs took possession of the jail. The ballot boxes were secured.

A count of the election results showed that the GI's candidate for sheriff, Knox Henry, had beaten Paul Cantrell by 1,168 votes to 789. Other GI candidates for Circuit Court Clerk, County Trustee and Register of Deeds won by similar margins.

In the aftermath, special deputies were appointed to maintain law and order and citizen patrols consisting of both GIs and citizens were appointed until the general election.

The "battle" attracted nationwide attention with extensive coverage in the *New York Times* and other publications. Both Chattanooga newspapers sent reporters to cover the unfolding story and both of them got heavily involved in the activities.

Times reporter, Richard Rogers, was seen mingling in the crowd as an outsider and was confronted by one of the ex-GIs and asked about his purpose for being in Athens. He was then escorted into a garage where four deputy sheriffs were being detained. One of the veterans used his wartime intimidation and humiliation tactics and threatened to shoot the deputies. Rogers was later released.

Veteran *News-Free Press* reporter J. B. Collins had a less friendly experience. He was carrying a camera and took an incriminating picture of a deputy sheriff removing a ballot box from one of the voting precincts and replacing it with an identical ballot box containing presumed pro-administration ballots. The original boxes were then taken to the jail for storage.

J. B. took a photo of the illegal exchange of the boxes, but his camera was abruptly seized, and the film was destroyed denying the printing of this historical picture. He also was incarcerated for about two hours in the county jail.

Reports of the National Guard being mobilized proved to be false as there was reluctance by both the Governor and State Adjutant General in calling out troops to possibly engage in combat with the ex-GIs who had just served their country.

The actions of the veterans in McMinn County was a motivating factor in the creation of the Good Government League in Chattanooga by Attorney Jac Chambliss and others to fight similar machine politics in Hamilton County.

The McMinn County War as depicted in the *New York Times*

Christmas Night Massacre in South Pittsburg (1927)

In 1927 the quiet joys of Christmas came to an abrupt halt as a result of a shootout in downtown South Pittsburg, Tennessee, on the night of December 25, 1927.

South Pittsburg during this period was the scene of bitter labor disputes involving union supporters and members and non-union advocates, for a period of approximately eight years. The City of South Pittsburg was born in 1873 on the west bank of Tennessee approximately thirty miles from the railroad hub of Chattanooga. The original plan was for the little town to grow in the stove industry into a major southern industrial city similar to Birmingham, Alabama.

In 1886, the Perry Stove Company based in Albany, New York, moved to South Pittsburg. As the result of management signing a national trade agreement with the International Molders Union of North America in 1891, South Pittsburg was heavily unionized. An anti-union company from Memphis, Tennessee, H. Wetter Manufacturing Company, bought the stove company and in the 1920's became the town of South Pittsburg's largest employer. Of the 2,500 residents, around 750 worked at Wetter. Approximately 75% of the work force were union members, and this percentage increased to around 90% after the agreement was signed. The plant gained a reputation of being a strong union shop, with Local 165 becoming the largest and oldest local of the Molders Union in the entire South.

In the 1920's-1930's, bitter labor disputes took place as the unions fought to preserve the status quo of the union shop (mandatory union membership) versus management efforts to adopt the open shop (voluntary union membership).

These ongoing efforts resulted in litigation in state courts in Marion County at Jasper and the federal district court in Chattanooga. Beginning in 1925, a number of stove manufacturers initiated a statewide effort to eliminate unions in the region. A number of strikes resulted in picket lines by the union, and petitions to enjoin the strikers from picketing and acts of violence, were sought by the companies. After a costly two-month strike, the company finally recognized one of the unions that had not been enjoined from setting up a picket line by the federal injunction. Union workers and supporters would not cross the picket and adversely affected the operation of the plant.

The conflicts that had divided the little town of South Pittsburg did not go away with the ending of the strike. Wetter Manufacturing announced that it was moving one of its plants to Gadsden, Alabama, because of poor labor conditions.

Law enforcement officials became heavily involved in the labor controversies. Pro union Sheriff of Marion County, Washington Coppinger, had defeated open shop supporter, Ben Parker, in 1926 in a bitter and hostile election that initially involved the issue of raiding moonshine whiskey stills but quickly involved the stove company labor dispute. Parker was subsequently hired as City Marshal in South Pittsburg.

On the night of December 25, 1927, a gunfight took place at the corner of Cedar Avenue and Third Street in downtown South Pittsburg which resulted in the death of both Sheriff Coppinger and Marshall Parker, in addition to four other law enforcement officers who were killed in the battle. Governor Henry Horton called in the Tennessee National Guard from Chattanooga to restore order. For several days, fifty soldiers patrolled the streets of South Pittsburg.

Although some parts of it are disputed by descendants of those involved in the events of 1927, a detailed eighteen page article by Barbara S. Haskew and Robert B. Jones written in 2001, titled "Labor Strike in the Southern Stove Industry – Shootout at South Pittsburg," is an excellent starting reference point covering the history of labor relations in Marion County and southeast Tennessee during the 1920's-1930's.

On July 20, 2014, the Tennessee Historical Society which was sponsored by the South Pittsburg Historical Preservation Society placed a two-sided historical marker near the scene of the Christmas night gunfight. The local society also maintains a history museum which includes memorabilia from this important chapter in the life of South Pittsburg, as well as artifacts from all other aspects of the town.

Whitwell Mine 21 Disaster
Gone But Not Forgotten

On December 8, 1981, the landscape and community of Whitwell, Tennessee, was changed forever as the result of the tragic explosion in Mine 21 that took the lives of thirteen men who worked at the site.

Coal had first been discovered in the area on the mountain by Thomas Wooten in 1852. Mining coal had been an important part of the way of life for many families in the area. It had provided a means of employment in the rural section on the north end of Marion County.

A difference of opinion existed between various miners as to whether the men working in the mines were paid a fair wage by the various companies or earned only a bare existence. The families of the miners primarily traded for their food and goods at company stores through script or tokens. Allegations of the company's taking advantage of the workers with inflated prices aroused dissension with some.

This dispute would culminate with labor unrest that led to the shooting of a United States Mine Workers Organizer in 1963. Feelings of pro-union versus pro-company often split the community for many years. The development of differences between management and the workers would be one of the contributing factors that would eventually lead to the cessation of coal mining operations.

Cheekville was the forerunner of the town Whitwell (established 1877.) The Tennessee Coal, Iron and Railroad Company that had set up a major mining operation in the northern end of Marion County. The success of the project led to the extension of the short line Sequatchie Valley Railroad being extended from Jasper to Whitwell in 1887. The primary function of the railroad was to transport coal to blast furnaces at South Pittsburgh and to other area industries. As a result, Whitwell became known as the "Coal City of the Sequatchie Valley."

However, on December 7, 1981, thirty coal miners entered Mine 21 to work their shift three miles into the mountain. They would continue working until around noon the next day, when a massive methane gas explosion took place that resulted in thirteen miners being killed. What followed was part of a state and federal investigation that led to the enactment of regulations resulting from several mining accidents taking place across the South in 1981 that claimed numerous lives.

Congressional hearings were conducted before the U.S. Senate Committee on Labor and Human Resource, chaired by Senator Ted Kennedy. The families of the deceased miners sued the companies for damages. The Department of Labor would find that the cause of the disaster was, "A cigarette lighter that was allowed to be taken into Mine 21, and when lit, it touched off the methane explosion" which caused the death of the miners. However, fault was also placed on a subsidiary of the owners, Grundy County Mining Company, for, "Failure to evacuate the men from a methane-laden mine shaft; to adequately ventilate said shaft; and not to vigorously force the federal regulation prohibitions on no smoking materials in the mine."

The mines closed in 1996 and the company declared bankruptcy in 1997.

Times have changed the economy in Whitwell. The residents are no longer dependent on coal to support their community. New industries have been created with more diversification of products, and workers do not have to rely solely on a job in the mines to survive economically.

However, the December 8, 1981, tragedy has not been forgotten. The Marion County Coal Miners Museum located at 300 A Main Street in Whitwell is a treasure trove of the history of mining in the region since its inception and demise. Retired miners and relatives eagerly passed on their knowledge and folklore of the past. It is open to the public free of charge, although donations are accepted, and its hours of operation are 8AM-4PM (CST) on Fridays and 8AM-12PM (CST) on Saturdays. The phone number is (423) 658-6868, and online information can be obtained at www.coalminersmuseum.com.

The tragedy has been preserved in song with the release of "Whitwell Mine" by Confederate Railroad singer, Danny Shirley, and Whitwell native and musician, Davey Smith, and his band The Pearl Snap Preachers. They also wrote and performed "Whitwell Mine 21" that depicts the December 8 disaster.

Recently a documentary film based on the event has been created. It was produced by students at the University of the South (Sewanee) and others. Kelsey Arbuckle, whose grandfather was one of the thirteen decedents, and Grundy County student, Alexa Fults, strongly felt that this important chapter of the mining history of Whitwell should be further preserved. They obtained the services of Sewanee Alumnus, Stephen Garret, to produce, and professor, Chris McDonough, to direct the film.

The film has already been shown in the Monteagle and Sewanee area and fills in many details on an important chapter in Whitwell's coal mining history.

A trailer of the film can be found at www.mine21.com.

Bloody Bledsoe
1863 & 1944

Bledsoe County, Tennessee, located on the northern end of the Sequatchie Valley on the Cumberland Plateau, acquired the title of "Bloody Bledsoe" primarily through two separate incidents. One originated in the Civil War and was followed by a violent and heinous crime committed approximately eighty years later in 1944.

In 1863, Bledsoe County was equally divided between supporters of the Union and the Confederacy. Two separate families were principal participants in the bloody feuds that originated in Sequatchie Valley. The Tolletts were Confederate sympathizers, while the Swaffords supported the Union.

John Tollett, Jr., age of 72, had become wealthy by acquiring over 10,000 acres of land and always carried a large amount of cash on his person. On April 30, 1863, John Jr. and another individual were killed by a group of robbers seeking his money cache. One member of the raiders was identified as Aaron Swafford.

This incident set off a series of bloody events between the two families that would continue over a period of approximately seventy years.

Perhaps the most famous of the feud incidents occurred on November 8, 1892, on election day, when both families confronted each other. Two Swaffords were killed, and three more, as well as a bystander, were wounded. One Tollett was stabbed repeatedly by a Swafford but survived.

A descendant on the Swafford side, Thomas V. Swafford, memorialized the famous feud in several books including one titled *The Swafford-Tollett Feud*.

Eventually the feud quieted down and the community attempted to eradicate itself of its violent past and to eliminate its reputation as "Bloody Bledsoe."

However, another separate ghastly incident took place on November 23, 1944, which was not related to the Tollett-Swafford feud, but nevertheless resurrected the community's reputation for violence.

The wife and daughter of the superintendent of the antiquated Tennessee State Reformatory, Henry Eugene Scott, were brutally murdered allegedly by a sixteen year old African-American inmate, James Scales, who was a trustee at the prison.

Mob violence ruled, and a group of vigilantes initially started to hang Scales, but an excited white individual shot him in the head multiple times, which prematurely ended the lynching. The death of the two women and the killing of the black youth at the remote correctional facility in Bledsoe County, Tennessee, at first became a national incident.

Although a public outcry was initiated with a reward of $500.00 pledged by Tennessee Governor Prentice Cooper for information leading to the capture and conviction of Scales' killers, no criminal prosecution was ever brought. In a few weeks, the heinous murders were quickly forgotten, because it was presumed that Scales was guilty of the crimes, and he had perished at the hands of the mob. The media quickly lost interest in the events.

Allegations have been made that both state and federal law enforcement authorities quickly withdrew from the case. When the Department of Justice and Federal Bureau of Investigation deferred to local and state Tennessee law agencies, the case quickly ended. Eventually no one was prosecuted for Scales' murder, although it was strongly alleged that guards and construction contractors employed by the state reformatory were involved in Scales' killing. No one was ever charged for the crime of his murder.

Future United State Supreme Court Justice and Assistant Attorney General, Tom C. Clark, probably erroneously claimed that no federal prosecution would be brought under the provisions of 18 U.S.C. 52, a Civil Rights statute used to prosecute lynching by persons "acting under the color of state law." He claimed it could not be applied because of a "lack of federal jurisdiction."

Legal scholars agree that the fact that employees of the reformatory and its hired contractors were allegedly involved would supply the legal requirement of "under color of state law."

Bledsoe County, like all communities, occasionally has had other crimes of violence, but hopefully the feud between the Tollett-Swafford families has passed into history.

Likewise the murders and the lynching of the teenager, James Scales, has been mostly forgotten.

A forty eight page article in Volume 19.2 of the *Texas Journal On Civil Liberties & Civil Rights* written by Andrew P. Cohen, titled "The Lynching of James Scales: How the FBI, the DOJ, and State Authorities Whitewashed Racial Violence in Bledsoe County, Tennessee" is an informative treatise on the life of Scales and the following events of the case. It was one of the darkest moments in the history of corrections in the State of Tennessee.

Conclusion

What started out as a search for adding some new excitement into my life after forty-eight years of an enjoyable law practice has become a joyous present of knowledge that I neglected in the days when I should have spent more time on other pursuits than just practicing law.

However, about forty of those years have been devoted to my relationship with Orange Grove Center and Tennessee Special Olympics.

If you enjoyed this book, get involved as a volunteer with either group. I promise that the unpaid rewards that you will received will be memorable.

The Author

Jerry H. Summers is a practicing attorney in Chattanooga, Tennessee. He has served as an assistant district attorney and municipal judge since he began his practice of law in 1966.

His entire life has been lived in Chattanooga, Tennessee except for seven years in St. Petersburg, Florida between the ages of seven and fourteen.

He has argued cases before the United States and Tennessee Supreme courts and has been involved in numerous landmark decisions in both civil and criminal law.

His peers in the legal profession have elected him to membership in the International Academy of Trial Lawyers, American College of Trial Lawyers, International Society of Barristers, American Board of Trail Advocates, American Board of Criminal Lawyers, and he has been selected every year since 1983 as one of the Best Lawyers in America, in both personal injury and criminal law.

By an unsolicited vote of the lawyers of Tennessee, he has consistently been selected as one of the "Best 100 Lawyers in Tennessee" and "Mid-South Super Lawyers".

Orange Grove Center and the Chattanooga Bar Association have both honored him as a Philanthropist of the Year for his community work. In 2007 he was selected as a Distinguished Alumnus at the Centennial Celebration of Central High School.

In 2014 he was honored by being designated as the Distinguished Alumnus at the University of the South at Sewanee, and in 2016 the University of Tennessee at Knoxville designated him as one of the Distinguished Alumni at that institution.

This is his sixth published work. His first literary attempt released in 2014 titled *The Turtle and the Lawyer* was an attempt to thank those individuals and entities that have helped him in life and to suggest respectfully that the reader do the same.

His second and third publications were a biography of the controversial life of Judge Raulston Schoolfield titled *Rush to Justice? Tennessee's Forgotten Trial of the Century – Schoolfield 1958,* and *Schoolfield:*

Out of the Ashes 1958-1982. A tribute to Central football Coach Stanley J. Farmer titled *We Called Him Coach* was his fourth publication. The story of the 1958 Chattanooga Central basketball team that lost the Tennessee State Championship Game by one point, entitled *One Shot Short,* is his fifth book.

Orange Grove Center, its staff and its clients are some of those that have had a profound effect on his life.

Index

A

Aaron, Hank 118
Abshire, David 61
Acree, Miriam 82
Adamsville 117
Adcock, Bonnie 129
Adcock, Herbert Grant 155, 156
Adhinion, L.T. 144
Adoption Scandal 7, 169, 171
African American Gentleman 6, 115
Alexander, Jr., Claude 161
Allison, June 169
Almon, Edward B. 102
Altamont 130
Altrock, Nick 112
American Temperance University 7, 133
Anderson, Joe 69
Anderson, Thomas "Tom" Jefferson 6, 90
André the Giant 158
Arbuckle, Kelsey 186
Armfield, John 130
Armstrong, John M. 167
Armstrong, Zella A. 167
Athens, Tennessee 5, **24**, 77, 180

B

Bachman, Nathan Lynn 6, 88
Baker, E.B. 134
Baker, Howard 57
Baker, Lamar 82
Banks, Ernie 118
Bartlett, Charles 5, 38
Baseball 6, 112
Bass, Mayor Ed 167
Bates, Finis L. 123
Battle of Athens 7, 180
Baylor School 6, 38, 90, 134, 166
Bean, Crawford 70
Bean, Joe 84
Bean, Russell 84

Beasley, I.D. 6, 92
Beckwith, Byron DeLa 6, 98
Beersheba Springs 6, 130
Behrens, Loretta "Little Iodine" 152
Bell, Raymond 176
Bell, Ed 176
Benefield, Charles 149
Berke, Mildred 159
Black, Joe 118
Blackmon, Harry 68
Blanton, Ray 54
Bledsoe County 7, 188
Bolt, George 153
Booth, Edwin 123
Booth, John Wilkes 6, 123
Boring, Robert 139
Bouch, Boshee 131
Boulware, Ben 149
Bouvier, Jacqueline 39
Boyd, Betty "Little Red" 153
Boyer, Ruth 160
Boy Named Sue 5, 48
Branum, Edith 153
Brasham, Midge "Toughie" 152
Brock, June 153
Brock, Ray 94
Brock, III, William (Bill) 80, 88
Btock, Jr., William E. 83
Brock, William Emerson 6, 83
Browning, Governor Gordon 170
Brown, William G. 173
Bryan, William Jennings 46
Burcham, Robert Wayne 155, 156
Burger, Warren 67
Burns, Robby 153
Burns, Sheriff Frank 175
Burritt College 6, 127
Bush, Rita 153
Bynum, C. Stephen 181

C

Cain, Beersheba Porter 130
Calvello, Ann 152
Campanella, Roy 118
Camp Campbell 138
Camp Crossville 7, 138
Camp Forrest 138
Camp Tyson 138
Cannon County 92
Cantor, Eddie 21
Cantrell, Paul 180
Capone, Al "Scarface" 5, 27
Carnes, William Davis 128
Carthage, Tennessee 92
Cartwright, J.P. 77
Case, H.B. 136
Cash, Joe 149
Cash, Johnny 47
Casteel, Bill 37
Catron, John 63
Chamberlain Field 7, 146
Chamberlain, Captain Hiram 146
Chamberlain, Morrow 146
Chambliss, Jac 182
Chattanooga Cherokees 7, 149
Chattanooga's Law School 6, 133
Chattanooga's Professional Football Team 7, 149
Chattanooga's Skaters 7, 152
Chitty, Arthur Ben 122
Christmas Night Massacre 7, 183
Civil Rights Advocate 5, 32
Clarksville, Tennessee 64
Clark, Tom C. 189
Clark, William F. 173
Clement, Frank G. 50
Cleveland, Tennessee 77, 106, 136, 155
Cleveland, President Grover 62
Clift, Anna Mae 5, 41
Clinton, Tennessee 36
Cohen, Andrew P. 190
Coleman, Joe 176
Collins, Eugene 69
Collins, J. B. 182
Cooley, Raymond H. 6, 75
Coolidge, Charles 77
Cooper, Governor Prentice 84, 189
Copperhill-McCaysville Adoption Scandal 7, 171
Coppinger, Washington 184
Corbell, Warren 113
Corn, Judy 160
Cosby, Bill 118
Cotton Ball 7, 167
Crawford, Joan 169
Crowe, Nathan 37
Crump, Edward Hull "Boss" 57, 85
Cumberland County 138
Cummings, Jim 6, 92
Cummings, Judge Will 167
Curriden, Mark 70

D

Daisy Mountain #1 7, 175
Daisy Mountain #2 7, 178
Dargue, W.L. 143
Darr, Leslie 57
Darrow, Clarence 46
Dayton, Tennessee 27
Dedman, Bill 38
DeLaughter, Bobby 99
Delorean, John Z. 162
Dillinger, John 122
Divorce Mill Scandal 7, 173
Dixon, Carl 109, 155
Dorsett, Tony 120
Doss, Desmond 77
Dow, Peggy 5, 24
Duke, Ray Eugene 6, 73
Dunlap, Tennessee 6, 75
Dwyer, William 35

E

Earnhardt, Dale 157
East, Jim 150

Eisenhower, President Dwight D. 38, 86
Elkins, Carl 132
Ellington, Governor Buford 54, 94
Engel, Joe 6, 112
Evans, Charles T. 133
Evers, Medgar 98

F

Fabris, Frank 149
Fairbanks, George 142
Fall, Albert F. 45
Farley, Jim 93
Federal District Judge Wilson 5, 57
Fentress County 71
Finlay, Carlos 125
Finney, Benjamin Ficklin 166
Finney, Dr. Ben 141
Fitzgerald, Jr. James (Jim) Thomas 6, 105
Flair, Ric 169
Fleischman, Chuck 82
Ford, President Gerald 59
Fortas, Abraham (Abe) 67
Frame, Buck 110
Frank H. McClung Museum 15
Franklin County 94, 141
Franks, Herschel P. 5, 54
Frazier, J.B. 80
Frederick, Tommy 177
Fryar, Freddy 155
Fryar, Jr., Harold 155
Fryar, Sr., Harold E. 155
Fuller, Drucilla 31
Fuller, Flop 37
Fults, Alexa 187

G

Gagne, Verne 158
Garland, Walter 174
Garret, Stephen 187
Garth, Ardena 97
Gehrig, Lou 113
George, Daniel E. 123
Godfrey, Arthur 175

Goldberg, Arthur 68
Gore, Albert 57
Gorgas, Dr. William C. 6, 125
Gorgas, Josiah 125
Gorgeous George 158
Gower, Herschel 132
Graham, Paul (Stump Daddy) 92
Grant, Ulysses S. 61
Grant University 133, 146
Green, Johnny 149
Griffin, Clark 112
Griffith, Calvin 113
Gruetli, Tennessee 131
Grundy County 130
Guerry, Alexander 134, 166
Guggenheim, Daniel 102
Guild, Virginia 168
Gulas, Nick 158

H

Hamilton County 70, 167
Hardin County 54
Harding, President Warren 66
Harlem Magicians 118
Harper, Samuel 107
Harriman, Tennessee 7, 135
Harris/Millsaps feud 175
Harrison, President Benjamin 62
Harris, Willie Lee 176
Haskew, Barbara S. 184
Hassler, Raymond "Friday" 155
Hayes, Joy 11
Hayes., President Rutherford 60
Haynes, Marquis 118
Haynes, Walter (Pete) 6, 92
Hefner, Hugh 42
Helen, John St. 123
Helmerich, Walter 25
Helmrich, Peggy Dow 26
Henley, Carey 150
Hennes, Gerhard G. 138
Henry County 138
Henry, Knox 181

Henry, Larry 163
Hicks Babies 172
Hicks, Dr. Thomas 172
Hicks., Herbert 46
Hicks, Judge Sue Kerr 5, 47
Hicks, Thomas 171
Higgins, Amy 163
Hixson, Ray 163
Hofa, Jimmy 28
Holmberg, Ruth 36
Holmes, Oliver Wendell 65
Hood, Robin 38
Hooker, John Jay 55
Hooks, Charlie 163
Hoover, J. Edgar 139
Hoppe, Bobby 151
Horton, Governor Henry 82, 184
Howell, Arch, III 159
Howell, Clark 32
Huff, Paul 77
Hull, Cordell 83
Huntington, Tennessee 89
H. Wetter Manufacturing Co. 183

J

Jackson, Howell Edmunds 62
Jamestown, Tennessee 72
Jasper, Tennessee 183
Jennings, Waylon 118
Jensen, Annie "Big Red" 152
John, Elton 118
Johnson, Ed 70
Johnson, Joe Lee 155
Johnson, Lucas 163
Johnson, President Andrew 60
Johnson, President Lyndon 33, 68
Johnson, Walter "Big Train" 112
Jones, Bob 121
Jones, Isaac Newton 128
Jones, Robert B. 184
Joyce, Eugene 57
Juhan, Bishop Frank 165

K

Kefauver, Carey Estes 6, 29
Kelley, Judge Camille 169
Kennedy, President John F. 33
Kennedy, Senator Ted 186
Kenyon, Nellie 5, 27
Key, Senator David McKendree 5, 60
Keyhoe, D.E. 103
King George V 126
King, Jr., Martin Luther 34
Kingston, Tennessee 44
Knoxville, Tennessee 57, 65, 92, 169
Kolwyck, Clarence 87, 173
Kupsky, Gregory 140

L

LaGuardia, Forello 35
Lanham, Marguerite 96
Law School 6, 133
Lea, Luke 83
Lebanon, Tennessee 62, 64, 92
Leguizamon, Harolene 178
Leinweber, Mike 149
Leitner, Jr., Paul 134
LeMay, General Curtis 90
Leming, Harrison 176
Lenoir, Elizabeth L. 61
Letner, Cotton 149
Liberace. 118
Lincoln, President Abraham 64
Lindbergh, Charles 6, 101, 103, 110
Little, Jessica 163
Littleton, Martin W. 5, 44
Lively, Jr., John L. 173
Lloyd, Marilyn 82
Lodge, Henry Cabot 86
Longley, David 149
Lovell Field 7, 101, 109, 143
Lovell, John 101
Love, Phillip R. 6, 103
"Lucky Lindy" 6, 101, 103, 110
Lurton, Horace Harmon 64
Lusk, Charles 96

M

Madisonville 84
Maidmont, C.C. 103
Majors, Bill 121
Majors, Bobby 121
Majors, Joe 120
Majors, Johnny 120
Majors, Larry 121
Majors, Shirley 120
Majors, Shirley Anne 121
Majors, The 6, 120
Makris, Patricia Short 122
Mansfield, Sherrif Pat 180
Marion County 18, 73, 97, 183
Marr Field 6, 7, 101, 103, 109, 143
Marr, Walter L. 101, 143
Mason, Gordon 150
Mays, Willie 118
McCallie, Dr. J.P. 82
McCallie School 32, 38, 146
McClure, James Thomas 110
McDaniel's, Revered 55
McDermott, Malcolm 49
McDonough, Chris 187
McGill, Ralph Emerson 5, 32
McKellar, Kenneth 89
McKenzie, Sr., Roy 133
McMinn County War 7, 180
McMinnville, Tennessee 5, 127
McReynolds, James Clark 66
McReynolds, Sam 85
Meacham, Ellis K. 5, 69
Meachem, Jon 38
Medal of Honor 6, 71, 73, 75, 79
Memphis, Tennessee 57, 62, 68, 92, 169, 183
Memphis Belle 5, 68
Mencken, H.L. 46
Miller, Judge 174
Mitchell, Jackie 113
Mitchell, James 107
Mix, Tom 5, 18
Moffat, John 51

Monteagle, Tennessee 5, 51
Monte, Ken 153
Montgomery, John David 22
Montgomery, Melissa Ann 22
Moolah, The Fabulous 159
Moonshine Feud – Daisy Mountain #1 7, 175
Moonshine Feud – Daisy Mountain #2 7, 178
Moore", A.C. "Scrappy 147
Moore, Colonel Richard 15
Moore, Grace 5, 15
Moore, Sr., James 15
Murphy, Audie 6, 80
Mushegan, Harry 178

N

Nashville, Tennessee 21, 55, 62, 66, 92, 138, 166
National Medal of Honor Heritage Center 79
Neal, John R. 5, 27
Neff, Thelma 98
Nelson, Willie 118
Newcombe, Don 118
News Reporter Extraordinaire 5, 27
Nightingale, Tennessee's 15
Nixon, President Richard 67, 82
Non-Motorized NASCAR 7, 161
Norman, Jack 56

O

Oak Ridge Boys 118
Oliver Springs, Tennessee 107
O'Neal, Judy 169
Orange Grove Center 3, 191
Orlowek, Nathaniel 122
Otey, Bishop James 130

P

Palermo, Mary Lou "Lulu" 153
Pall Mall, Tennessee 71
Panama Canal 6, 124

Paris, Tennessee 62
Parker, Alton B. 44
Parker/Ashley Feud 175
Parker, Ben 184
Parker, Mrs. Theodore 176
Parker, Theodore "Pap" 175
Parker, William L. "Boots" 176
Paty, Selma (Sunny) Cash 55, 97
Payne, Louisa Price 122
Payne, Phil 147
Pearman, Charles "Duke" 6, 77
Pearson, Drew 67
Perry Stove Company 183
Petty, George 42
Phillips, Leroy, Jr. 70
Pickett County 83
Pierce, President Franklin 131
Pioneer In Journalism And Media 5, 29
Pioneer of the Cumberlands 6, 127
Pioneer Women Attorneys 6, 96
Polk, Bishop Leonidas 130, 142
Polk, James 131
Popham, John N., III 5, 35
Porter, Harry G. 6, 105
Porter, Governor James D. 60
POW camps 138
Powell, Dick 169
Prater, Raymond 6, 79
Presley, Elvis 118
Pritchard, Robert 133
Pulitzer Prize Winner 5, 38

Q

Quintard, Charles T. 141

R

Ragan, Charles O. 149
Rash, Charlie 121
Raulston-Arlens, Jobyna 5, 18
Raulston, John 46
Rawls, Wendell 38
Ray, James Earl 55
Rechichar, Bert 150

Reece, B. Carroll 85
Reed, Major Walter 125
Reynolds, Burt 22
Rhea County 46
Richard City, Tennessee 75
Richey, Robert 155
Richey, Sheriff Rex 175
Richy, Frank 136
Roane County 135
Robbins, Mickey 13
Roberts, Jake 160
Robinson, Jackie 107
Rogers, Richard 181
Roller Derby 7, 152
Rolling Stones 118
Roosevelt, Eleanor 170
Roosevelt, President Franklin
   Delano 67
Roosevelt, President Theodore 44
Runyon, Damon 152
Rupp, Adolph 117
Ruth, Babe 113

S

Sanford, Edward Terry 65
Saperstein, Abe 118
Satterfield, Bob 153
Savannah, Tennessee 54
Scales, James 189
Scanland, Opal 96
Schardt, Al 112
Schoolfield, Raulston 56
Scopes, John T. 46
Scopes "Monkey" trial 5, 27, 46
Scott, Dred 63
Scott, Henry Eugene 189
Scott, Myron E. (Scottie) 161
Scruggs, Richard "Dickie" 100
Seltzer, Leo 152
Sewanee 7, 52, 115, 117, 120, 122, 125,
   141, 165, 187
Sewanee Football 7, 165
Shackelford, Rufus 90

Sharp, George 42
Shepherd, Lewis 133
Shields, John Knight 88
Shipp, Joseph 65
Shirley, Danny 186
Shore, Dinah 5, 21
Signal Mountain, Tennessee 6, 98
Silverstein, Shel 47
Sims, Willie 6, 115
Sinclair, Harry Ford 45
Sitton, Claude F. 36
Six, Willie 6, 115
Sizer, J.B. 84
Skillern, Fred 43
Smalley, Peggy 153
Smartt, Red 153
Smartt, Vaughn 173
Smartt, William "Red" 153
Smith, Davey 186
Smith, Drue 5, 29
Smith, Steve 43
Soap Box Derby 7, 161
Soddy,Daisy Tennessee 5, 34, 41, 146, 155, 179
Sonny & Cher 118
South Pittsburg, Tennessee 7, 18, 75, 92, 105, 183, 185
Sparta, Tennessee 127
Spencer, Tennessee 129
Sprowls, Jesse 48
Stephenson, Governor Adali 86
Stevenson, Ashton 164
Stewart, Chase 164
Stewart, Michael 163
Stewart, Parker 164
Stinson, Eddie 143
Stock Car Racing History 7, 155
Stophel, John 134
Suggs, Will 163
Swafford, Aaron 188
Swafford, Claude 97
Swafford, Thomas V. 188
Swaney, W.B. 133

T

Taft, President William Howard 65
Talbott, Harold E. 38
Talmadge, Herman 33
Tann, Georgia 169
Tatum, Goose 118
Ten Mile, Tennessee 149
Tennessee Adoption Scandal 7, 169
Tennessee Football Family 6, 120
Tennessee Nightingale 5, 15
Tennessee's Unholy Trinity 6, 92
Tennessee U.S. Supreme Court Justices 5, 62
Thaw, Harry 45
The Crosses at Sewanee 7, 141
Thesz, Lou 158
Thomas, Neil, Jr. 58
Thornton, Harry 158
Thrasher, Jr., Wilkes T. 80
Tollett, Jr., John 188
Travis, Ron 76
Trigg, Connally F. 61
Trout, Ann Hale 132
Truman, President Harry S. 33, 86, 107
Trusley, George 176
Turkey Day Football 7, 146
Turner, Lana 169
Turner, Robert 162
Tuskegee Airman 6, 107
Twain, Mark 60
Tyson, Lawrence D. 82

U

Unholy Trinity 6, 92
U.S. Supreme Court Justices 5, 62

V

Van Buren County 127
Van Buren, President Martin 63
Varga Girl 42
Vargas, Alberto 41
Varnell, Lon Shelton 6, 117
Varner, Vic 150
Vass, Chris 13
Veeck, Bill 112

W

Walker, James 35
Walker, Nick 11
Wallace, Governor George C. 90, 158
Wamp, Congressman Zach 82
Warren, Justice Earl 68
Wayne, Brett 160
Weathers, Tom 151
Weill, Harry 173
Weintal., Edward 40
Welch, Ray 158
Welk, Lawrence 118
West, Marian 129
Weston, Joan 152
White, Hugh Lawson 63
White, Joseph C. 6, 107
White, Sanford 45
Whitwell Mine Disaster 7, 183
Whitwell, Tennessee 6, 73, 183
Wilcox, David 176
Williams, Mary Louise 98
Williams, Myrlie Evers 98
Willie Six 115
Wilson, Emmett 149
Wilson, Frank Wiley 5, 57
Wilson, Jack 153
Wilson, John 13 , 122
Wilson, President Woodrow 66, 88, 126
Winchester, Tennessee 5, **21**, 92
Wolfson, Lewis 68
Woodbury, Tennessee 92
Wood, Gus A., Jr. 173
Wooten, Thomas 185
Wrestling or "Rassling" 7, 158

Y

Yamamoto, Tojo 159
Yeager, Chuck 105
York, Clyde 138
York, Sgt. Alvin 5, 71

Z

Ziegfeld, Florenz 42

www.ingramcontent.com/pod-product-compliance
Lightning Source LLC
Chambersburg PA
CBHW070536170426
43200CB00011B/2444